MATH

Grade 3

Thomas J. Richards
Mathematics Teacher
Lamar Junior-Senior High School
Lamar, Missouri

SPECTRUM

Grand Rapids, Michigan

Photo Credits
Tony Freeman, 124; Glencoe staff photo, 50, 88;
Jeff Greenberg, 102; Brent Jones, 2; Dan Witt, 60, 80

Frank Schaffer Publications®

Spectrum is an imprint of Frank Schaffer Publications.

Send all inquiries to:
Frank Schaffer Publications
3195 Wilson Drive NW
Grand Rapids, Michigan 49534

Math—grade 3

ISBN 1-56189-903-8

8 9 10 11 12 13 VHG 11 10 09 08 07 06

Table of Contents

The SPECTRUM

Contents

MATHEMATICS Series
of Units

SPECTRUM MATHEMATICS is a non-graded, consumable series for students who need special help with the basic skills of computation and problem solving. This successful series emphasizes skill development and practice, without complex terminology or abstract symbolism. Because of the nature of the content and the students for whom the series is intended, readability has been carefully controlled to comply with the mathematics level of each book.

Features:

- A **Pre-Test** at the beginning of each chapter helps determine a student's understanding of the chapter content. The Pre-Test enables students and teachers to identify specific skills that need attention.
- **Developmental exercises** are provided at the top of the page when new skills are introduced. These exercises involve students in learning and serve as an aid for individualized instruction or independent study.
- **Abundant opportunities for practice** follow the developmental exercises.
- **Problem-solving pages** enable students to apply skills to realistic problems they will meet in everyday life.

- A **Test** at the end of each chapter gives students and teachers an opportunity to check understanding. A **Mid-Book Test**, covering Chapters 1–6, and a **Final Test**, covering all chapters, provide for further checks of understanding.
- A **Record of Test Scores** is provided on page xvi of this book so students can chart their progress as they complete each chapter test.
- **Answers** to all problems and test items are included at the back of the book.

This is the third edition of *SPECTRUM MATHEMATICS*. The basic books have remained the same. Some new, useful features have been added.

New Features:

- **Scope and Sequence Charts** for the entire Spectrum Mathematics series are included on pages iv–v.
- **Basic Facts Tests** for addition, subtraction, multiplication, and division are included on pages vii–xiv. There are two forms of each test. These may be given at any time the student or teacher decides they are appropriate.
- An **Assignment Record Sheet** is provided on page xv.

Addition Facts (Form A)

	a	*b*	*c*	*d*	*e*	*f*	*g*	*h*
1.	3 +1	8 +2	1 +6	4 +7	6 +3	2 +8	4 +5	7 +9
2.	6 +4	1 +8	3 +9	2 +1	5 +0	0 +2	9 +1	3 +2
3.	2 +7	6 +9	4 +8	9 +3	2 +2	8 +0	0 +4	7 +1
4.	5 +2	8 +3	1 +5	7 +8	6 +2	4 +6	5 +4	9 +4
5.	2 +3	9 +0	4 +3	2 +9	1 +1	8 +8	3 +5	5 +7
6.	8 +9	3 +3	9 +5	6 +6	3 +8	0 +6	7 +3	2 +6
7.	7 +7	4 +1	3 +6	8 +7	0 +0	9 +8	9 +2	7 +5
8.	2 +4	0 +3	5 +8	2 +5	1 +9	1 +0	5 +9	8 +4
9.	6 +7	3 +4	9 +9	0 +7	8 +5	7 +4	5 +6	3 +7
10.	9 +7	8 +6	5 +5	7 +6	6 +8	6 +5	4 +9	9 +6

Perfect score: 80   My score: _____

Addition Facts (Form B)

	a	*b*	*c*	*d*	*e*	*f*	*g*	*h*
1.	8 +2	7 +0	0 +1	1 +1	6 +4	5 +2	4 +9	2 +7
2.	1 +0	6 +3	3 +0	2 +3	7 +1	8 +1	6 +5	1 +9
3.	0 +5	1 +2	6 +6	3 +5	9 +5	5 +7	7 +6	3 +8
4.	4 +2	6 +8	8 +5	2 +6	5 +8	9 +8	0 +0	4 +4
5.	7 +2	9 +7	0 +8	4 +7	7 +9	5 +9	3 +3	5 +4
6.	1 +3	9 +0	2 +2	5 +1	7 +7	6 +0	8 +6	9 +4
7.	4 +8	9 +3	1 +4	2 +9	9 +2	8 +3	7 +3	0 +9
8.	2 +0	2 +8	8 +4	4 +0	8 +7	9 +1	4 +3	5 +5
9.	8 +9	5 +6	6 +1	1 +7	4 +6	7 +5	9 +9	6 +7
10.	3 +9	9 +6	7 +8	5 +3	6 +9	8 +8	7 +4	3 +7

Perfect score: 80   My score: _____

Subtraction Facts (Form A)

	a	*b*	*c*	*d*	*e*	*f*	*g*	*h*
1.	1 1 −3	8 −4	5 −5	1 2 −3	2 −1	1 0 −9	4 −3	1 1 −9
2.	1 0 −5	3 −3	6 −3	1 1 −4	7 −6	1 0 −6	9 −2	1 2 −4
3.	1 6 −7	9 −0	5 −4	1 3 −7	1 0 −2	1 5 −9	8 −8	1 4 −5
4.	1 3 −8	4 −2	7 −7	1 2 −9	2 −0	1 7 −9	6 −1	1 1 −7
5.	1 8 −9	9 −8	6 −4	1 1 −5	3 −1	1 5 −7	9 −9	1 0 −8
6.	1 2 −6	8 −7	3 −2	1 3 −9	1 0 −4	1 4 −6	7 −5	1 2 −5
7.	1 5 −8	8 −3	9 −5	1 2 −8	8 −6	1 6 −9	5 −3	1 2 −7
8.	1 4 −7	7 −1	6 −5	1 1 −6	4 −1	1 0 −7	1 −1	1 0 −3
9.	1 3 −4	0 −0	8 −0	1 6 −8	9 −7	1 4 −9	6 −6	1 3 −6
10.	1 7 −8	9 −6	7 −4	1 5 −6	1 1 −2	1 3 −5	9 −3	1 4 −8

Perfect score: 80   My score: _____

Subtraction Facts (Form B)

	a	*b*	*c*	*d*	*e*	*f*	*g*	*h*
1.	4 −2	1 3 −7	3 −2	1 0 −1	6 −5	8 −1	1 4 −5	1 0 −7
2.	8 −2	1 2 −5	6 −3	1 0 −8	2 −1	1 1 −9	1 4 −8	1 1 −2
3.	4 −0	1 1 −3	9 −1	1 5 −6	5 −0	7 −1	1 3 −8	1 0 −9
4.	6 −4	1 3 −9	1 −0	9 −2	7 −3	1 2 −4	1 5 −7	5 −4
5.	0 −0	1 2 −3	8 −4	1 4 −6	8 −5	1 0 −4	1 6 −9	1 1 −6
6.	9 −9	1 0 −2	3 −2	1 5 −9	5 −1	1 2 −9	1 4 −9	1 0 −3
7.	7 −5	1 2 −7	7 −0	1 4 −7	7 −2	1 1 −4	1 6 −7	1 1 −5
8.	4 −4	1 3 −6	5 −2	1 6 −8	9 −4	1 0 −5	1 3 −4	6 −0
9.	8 −3	1 2 −6	1 −1	1 8 −9	4 −3	1 2 −8	1 4 −6	1 3 −5
10.	9 −6	1 1 −7	8 −8	1 7 −8	6 −2	1 0 −6	1 7 −9	1 5 −8

Perfect score: 80   My score: _____

Multiplication Facts (Form A)

	a	b	c	d	e	f	g	h
1.	2 ×2	6 ×3	0 ×1	3 ×2	8 ×0	1 ×1	7 ×1	8 ×4
2.	7 ×4	3 ×0	8 ×3	2 ×1	5 ×1	3 ×6	2 ×5	6 ×2
3.	3 ×7	5 ×5	8 ×6	6 ×0	4 ×9	9 ×1	7 ×2	4 ×3
4.	8 ×5	2 ×4	7 ×5	4 ×1	8 ×2	6 ×5	7 ×8	1 ×9
5.	4 ×0	8 ×1	9 ×3	5 ×6	3 ×8	2 ×9	5 ×7	9 ×2
6.	7 ×9	6 ×4	4 ×8	7 ×3	6 ×9	9 ×4	2 ×6	8 ×7
7.	1 ×3	9 ×5	5 ×3	8 ×8	4 ×5	0 ×7	3 ×4	7 ×6
8.	3 ×5	9 ×0	2 ×7	7 ×7	5 ×8	9 ×6	2 ×0	6 ×6
9.	9 ×9	1 ×8	6 ×8	0 ×0	9 ×7	0 ×5	3 ×9	8 ×9
10.	4 ×6	9 ×8	2 ×8	4 ×7	1 ×6	6 ×7	3 ×3	5 ×9

Perfect score: 80   My score: _____

Multiplication Facts (Form B)

	a	*b*	*c*	*d*	*e*	*f*	*g*	*h*
1.	2 ×2	6 ×4	4 ×1	7 ×7	1 ×0	2 ×9	0 ×2	1 ×4
2.	5 ×0	3 ×1	8 ×3	3 ×9	0 ×9	9 ×6	7 ×3	4 ×8
3.	1 ×2	4 ×9	6 ×3	7 ×2	5 ×7	1 ×5	2 ×8	8 ×2
4.	8 ×4	9 ×5	4 ×2	2 ×3	6 ×9	4 ×7	4 ×3	5 ×6
5.	2 ×4	7 ×1	3 ×3	6 ×2	9 ×4	5 ×1	6 ×8	7 ×6
6.	7 ×4	1 ×1	5 ×8	8 ×5	7 ×0	0 ×8	6 ×1	9 ×3
7.	3 ×8	9 ×7	5 ×2	2 ×6	3 ×4	8 ×9	7 ×5	6 ×7
8.	8 ×6	5 ×4	4 ×6	9 ×2	1 ×7	8 ×1	4 ×4	3 ×5
9.	6 ×5	7 ×8	9 ×9	0 ×0	3 ×7	5 ×5	2 ×5	8 ×8
10.	9 ×1	4 ×5	8 ×7	6 ×6	9 ×8	7 ×9	2 ×7	5 ×9

Perfect score: 80   My score: _____

Division Facts (Form A)

NAME _____

	a	b	c	d	e	f	g
1.	7)7	4)2 4	9)1 8	3)1 8	8)3 2	6)1 2	2)8
2.	8)0	1)9	5)1 5	2)1 6	7)2 1	5)0	8)8
3.	3)1 5	8)4 0	7)2 8	4)2 0	7)6 3	3)2 1	9)3 6
4.	7)1 4	5)2 0	6)6	2)1 8	6)2 4	1)2	2)1 0
5.	8)2 4	5)1 0	4)2 8	9)4 5	1)8	5)4 5	8)4 8
6.	5)4 0	6)3 0	1)6	5)5	9)0	8)1 6	4)4
7.	9)5 4	1)5	7)5 6	6)1 8	4)1 6	6)5 4	3)6
8.	7)3 5	3)1 2	2)0	8)5 6	2)1 2	6)0	7)4 9
9.	4)0	8)6 4	5)3 5	4)3 2	3)2 4	1)3	6)3 6
10.	6)4 2	9)9	4)8	1)0	9)6 3	4)1 2	5)2 5
11.	3)9	2)1 4	9)7 2	7)4 2	2)4	8)7 2	1)1
12.	9)8 1	6)4 8	4)3 6	2)6	5)3 0	1)4	3)2 7

Perfect score: 84   My score: _____

xiii

Division Facts (Form B)

	a	b	c	d	e	f	g
1.	2)2	4)12	3)9	6)24	8)48	3)6	8)0
2.	6)30	9)36	7)14	2)4	5)5	5)40	7)63
3.	1)7	5)0	5)45	9)45	4)8	1)9	8)56
4.	3)3	4)16	7)56	5)35	8)8	4)4	9)54
5.	7)0	3)12	8)64	6)36	7)21	2)6	4)36
6.	9)27	2)8	6)18	9)0	6)54	1)0	6)12
7.	6)0	4)20	8)40	1)1	8)72	3)15	5)30
8.	9)18	5)25	7)49	4)24	3)24	9)63	2)10
9.	3)0	9)9	6)48	2)14	6)6	1)6	8)16
10.	3)18	7)35	1)4	9)72	4)28	2)12	7)42
11.	1)8	8)32	5)20	5)10	2)18	6)42	5)15
12.	8)24	3)21	9)81	2)16	7)28	3)27	4)32

Perfect score: 84   My score: _____

Assignment Record Sheet

NAME _____

Pages Assigned	Date	Score	Pages Assigned	Date	Score	Pages Assigned	Date	Score

SPECTRUM MATHEMATICS

Record of Test Scores

Rank	Test Pages														
	17	29	41	57	67	75	85	95	105	115	125	133	144	145-6	147–50
Excellent	50	25	25	25	25	20	25	25	25	25	29 / 25	15	19	40	60
Very Good	40	20	20	20	20	15	20	20	20	20			15 / 30		50
Good	30	15	15	15	15	10	15	15	15	15	20 / 15	10	10	20	40 / 30
Fair	20	10	10	10	10		10	10	10	10	10	5			20
Poor	10	5	5	5	5	5	5	5	5	5	5		5	10	10
	0	0	0	0	0	0	0	0	0	0	0	0	0	0	0

To record the score you receive on a TEST:

(1) Find the vertical scale below the page number of that TEST,
(2) on that vertical scale, draw a ● at the mark which represents your score.

For example, if your score for the TEST on page 17 is "My score: 32," draw a ● at the 32-mark on the first vertical scale. A score of 32 would show that your rank is "Good." You can check your progress from one test to the next by connecting the dots with a line segment.

PRE-TEST—Addition and Subtraction

Add.

	a	*b*	*c*	*d*	*e*	*f*
1.	2 +8	7 +5	9 +4	5 +5	6 +8	8 +9
2.	4 +7	8 +5	6 +4	9 +9	1 +9	8 +7
3.	8 +8	9 +5	6 +7	7 +3	4 +8	9 +3
4.	3 +8	6 +6	9 +2	7 +7	9 +7	6 +9

Subtract.

	a	*b*	*c*	*d*	*e*	*f*
5.	1 0 − 3	1 2 − 8	1 5 − 6	1 4 − 5	1 8 − 9	1 6 − 8
6.	1 3 − 5	1 2 − 4	1 6 − 7	1 0 − 2	1 1 − 7	1 4 − 6
7.	1 0 − 5	1 2 − 6	1 1 − 2	1 5 − 7	1 7 − 9	1 0 − 8
8.	1 2 − 5	1 0 − 1	1 3 − 4	1 7 − 8	1 1 − 3	1 0 − 6
9.	1 2 − 9	1 5 − 8	1 6 − 9	1 1 − 5	1 3 − 6	1 4 − 7

Perfect score: 54   My score: _____

Problem-Solving Pre-Test

Solve each problem.

1. Two adults and two children are playing. How many people are playing?

1.

There are _____ adults.

There are _____ children.

There are _____ people playing.

2. The Durhams played football for 1 hour and then played baseball for 2 hours. How many hours did they play in all?

2.

They played football for _____ hour.

They played baseball for _____ hours.

They played _____ hours in all.

3. The Durhams' house has 5 bedrooms in all. There are 2 bedrooms downstairs. The rest of the bedrooms are upstairs. How many bedrooms are upstairs?

3.

There are _____ bedrooms in all.

There are _____ bedrooms downstairs.

There are _____ bedrooms upstairs.

Perfect score: 9   My score: _____

2

Lesson 1   Addition

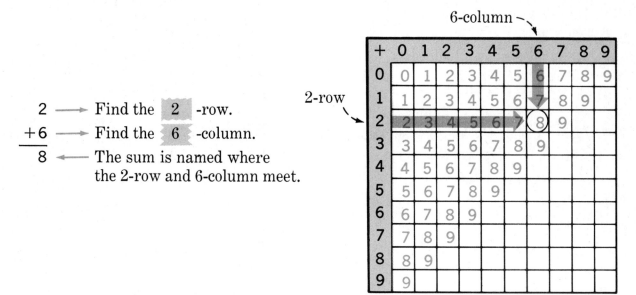

2 ——→ Find the 2 -row.

+6 ——→ Find the 6 -column.

8 ←—— The sum is named where
the 2-row and 6-column meet.

Add.

	a	*b*	*c*	*d*	*e*	*f*	*g*	*h*
1.	2 +4	3 +1	1 +2	7 +0	0 +4	1 +4	5 +2	3 +3
2.	2 +0	6 +3	4 +4	3 +0	5 +3	1 +6	0 +5	8 +1
3.	2 +6	1 +0	1 +5	2 +2	3 +2	2 +1	5 +4	1 +7
4.	9 +0	5 +1	0 +3	4 +1	4 +5	1 +8	8 +0	4 +3
5.	0 +0	2 +3	7 +1	0 +9	4 +2	0 +2	0 +7	1 +1
6.	2 +7	0 +1	6 +2	0 +6	1 +3	6 +1	6 +0	7 +2

Perfect score: 48   My score: _____

Lesson 2   Subtraction

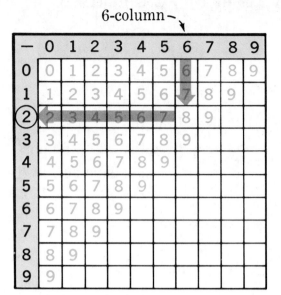

6-column

8 → Find 8 in

−6 → the **6**-column.

‾‾2 ← The difference is named in the ▨ at the end of this row.

Subtract.

	a	b	c	d	e	f	g	h
1.	5 −4	3 −2	7 −7	1 −0	8 −2	9 −7	4 −3	6 −1
2.	7 −2	2 −2	7 −6	8 −7	9 −3	9 −8	4 −1	6 −0
3.	0 −0	7 −1	3 −0	6 −6	4 −2	6 −2	9 −5	8 −6
4.	9 −9	8 −4	9 −1	7 −5	7 −4	6 −5	2 −0	1 −1
5.	3 −1	9 −4	7 −3	5 −2	5 −1	6 −4	4 −4	8 −1
6.	5 −5	2 −1	5 −0	8 −3	9 −0	6 −3	7 −0	5 −3

Perfect score: 48   My score: _____

Lesson 3 Addition

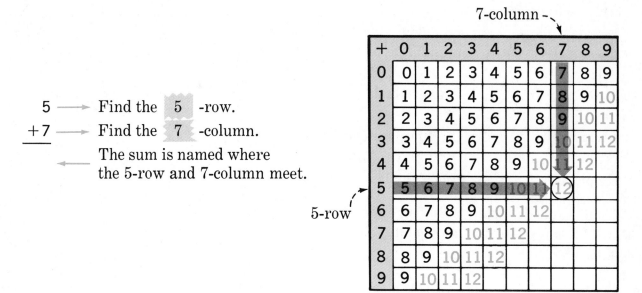

5 ⟶ Find the 5 -row.

+7 ⟶ Find the 7 -column.

⟵ The sum is named where the 5-row and 7-column meet.

7-column

5-row

Add.

	a	b	c	d	e	f
1.	6 +5	7 +3	2 +7	8 +4	9 +2	6 +3
2.	8 +2	3 +9	3 +5	5 +2	6 +4	5 +5
3.	5 +3	9 +3	6 +6	3 +7	4 +7	9 +1
4.	5 +7	8 +1	5 +6	2 +8	2 +5	7 +5
5.	3 +4	4 +5	4 +6	2 +9	8 +3	4 +8
6.	2 +6	1 +9	3 +8	7 +1	7 +4	6 +2

Perfect score: 36   My score: _____

Problem Solving

Solve each problem.

1. Andy played 2 games today. He played 9 games yesterday. How many games did he play in all?

Andy played _____ games today.

Andy played _____ games yesterday.

He played _____ games in all.

2. Jane rode her bicycle 8 kilometers yesterday. She rode 4 kilometers today. How many kilometers did she ride in all?

Jane rode _____ kilometers yesterday.

Jane rode _____ kilometers today.

Jane rode _____ kilometers in all.

3. Paul hit the ball 7 times. He missed 4 times. How many times did he swing at the ball?

Paul hit the ball _____ times.

Paul missed the ball _____ times.

Paul swung at the ball _____ times.

4. There were 4 people in a room. Six more people came in. How many people were in the room then?

_____ people were in a room.

_____ more people came in.

_____ people were in the room then.

5. Paula and Alice each read 6 books. How many books did they read in all?

They read _____ books in all.

1.
2.
3.

4.	5.

Perfect score: 13   My score: _____

6

Lesson 4   Subtraction

NAME _____

4-column

−	0	1	2	3	4	5	6	7	8	9
0	0	1	2	3	4	5	6	7	8	9
1	1	2	3	4	5	6	7	8	9	10
2	2	3	4	5	6	7	8	9	10	11
3	3	4	5	6	7	8	9	10	11	12
4	4	5	6	7	8	9	10	11	12	
5	5	6	7	8	9	10	11	12		
6	6	7	8	9	10	11	12			
7	7	8	9	10	11	12				
8	8	9	10	11	12					
9	9	10	11	12						

11 → Find 11 in

−4 → the 4 -column.

← The difference is named in the at the end of this row.

Subtract.

	a	b	c	d	e	f
1.	11 − 7	10 − 4	10 − 8	12 − 9	8 −5	11 − 2
2.	10 − 1	11 − 8	7 −4	11 − 6	12 − 3	9 −6
3.	12 − 7	10 − 7	9 −3	11 − 9	12 − 4	10 − 5
4.	8 −6	12 − 8	9 −5	10 − 6	11 − 5	8 −8
5.	12 − 6	10 − 9	9 −8	7 −6	11 − 4	9 −7
6.	10 − 2	7 −3	10 − 3	12 − 5	8 −3	11 − 3

Perfect score: 36   My score: _____

Problem Solving

Solve each problem.

1. There were 12 nails in a box. Willy used 3 of them. How many nails are still in the box?

_____ nails were in a box.

_____ nails were used.

_____ nails are still in the box.

2. There are 11 checkers on a board. Eight of them are black. The rest are red. How many red checkers are on the board?

_____ checkers are on a board.

_____ checkers are black, and the rest are red.

_____ red checkers are on the board.

3. Marty is 10 years old. Her brother Larry is 7. Marty is how many years older than Larry?

Marty's age is _____ years.

Larry's age is _____ years.

Marty is _____ years older than Larry.

4. Joy walked 11 blocks. Ann walked 2 blocks. Joy walked how much farther than Ann?

Joy walked _____ blocks.

Ann walked _____ blocks.

Joy walked _____ blocks farther than Ann.

5. Twelve people are in a room. Five of them are men. How many are women?

_____ women are in the room.

1.	
2.	
3.	
4.	**5.**

Lesson 5   Addition and Subtraction

To check	5 ↖		To check	13 ↖	
$5+6=11$,	$+6$	These should	$13-4=9$,	-4	These should
subtract 6	$\overline{11}$	be the same.	add 4	$\overline{9}$	be the same.
from 11.	-6		to _____.	$+4$	
	$\overline{5}$ ↙			$\overline{13}$ ↙	

Add. Check each answer.

	a	b	c	d	e	f
1.	2 $+9$	8 $+4$	7 $+3$	3 $+8$	1 $+9$	6 $+6$
2.	9 $+3$	5 $+6$	4 $+8$	5 $+5$	7 $+4$	9 $+1$

Subtract. Check each answer.

3.	1 0 $-\ 8$	1 2 $-\ 7$	1 1 $-\ 3$	1 0 $-\ 4$	1 1 $-\ 7$	1 0 $-\ 7$
4.	1 1 $-\ 9$	1 2 $-\ 8$	1 1 $-\ 8$	1 2 $-\ 5$	1 0 $-\ 6$	1 0 $-\ 3$

Perfect score: 24   My score: _____

Problem Solving

Answer each question.

1. Ben had some marbles. He gave 2 of them away and had 9 left. How many marbles did he start with?

Are you to add
or subtract? _____

How many marbles did he start with? _____

2. A full box has 10 pieces of chalk. This box has only 8 pieces. How many pieces are missing?

Are you to add
or subtract? _____

How many pieces are missing? _____

3. Jack is 11 years old today. How old was he 4 years ago?

Are you to add
or subtract? _____

How old was Jack 4 years ago? _____

4. Nine boys were playing ball. Then 3 more boys began to play. How many boys were playing ball then?

Are you to add
or subtract? _____

How many boys were playing then? _____

5. Millie has as many sisters as brothers. She has 5 brothers. How many brothers and sisters does she have?

Are you to add
or subtract? _____

How many brothers and
sisters does Millie have? _____

6. Tricia invited 12 people to her party. Seven people came. How many people that were invited did not come?

Are you to add
or subtract? _____

How many people did not come? _____

1.

2.

3.

4.

5.

6.

Perfect score: 12   My score: _____

10

Lesson 6 Addition

6 → Find the **6**-row.
+7 → Find the **7**-column.
The sum is named where the
6-row and 7-column meet.

9 → Find the **9**-row.
+8 → Find the **8**-column.
The sum is named where the
9-row and 8-column meet.

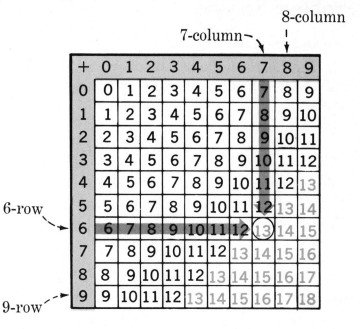

Add.

	a	b	c	d	e	f
1.	7 +6	8 +7	7 +4	9 +7	4 +9	8 +8
2.	5 +9	6 +4	6 +8	5 +8	8 +4	7 +8
3.	6 +9	5 +5	6 +7	9 +2	8 +6	4 +6
4.	5 +7	8 +9	9 +6	5 +6	9 +4	9 +9
5.	7 +9	8 +2	9 +8	8 +5	9 +1	4 +7
6.	9 +5	6 +6	2 +9	4 +8	7 +7	9 +3

Perfect score: 36   My score: _____

11

Problem Solving

Solve each problem.

1. Ellen worked 9 hours Monday. She worked 7 hours Tuesday. How many hours did she work in all on those two days?

She worked _____ hours Monday.

She worked _____ hours Tuesday.

She worked _____ hours in all on those two days.

2. Frank has 6 windows to wash. Janet has 9 windows to wash. How many windows do they have to wash in all?

Frank has _____ windows to wash.

Janet has _____ windows to wash.

Together they have _____ windows to wash.

3. Seven cars are in the first row. Six cars are in the second row. How many cars are in the first two rows?

_____ cars are in the first two rows.

4. There are 9 men and 8 women at work. How many people are at work?

There are _____ people at work.

5. Phil worked 8 hours. Geraldo worked the same number of hours. How many hours did Phil and Geraldo work in all?

They worked _____ hours in all.

6. There are 6 plants in a box. Seven more are on a table. How many plants are there?

There are _____ plants.

1.

2.

3.

4.

5.

6.

Perfect score: 10   My score: _____

12

Lesson 7   Subtraction

6-column ⌐   8-column ⌐

13 ⟶ Find 13 in
−8 ⟶ the [8]-column.
The difference is named in the ▨ at the end of that row.

15 ⟶ Find 15 in
−6 ⟶ the [6]-column.
The difference is named in the ▨ at the end of that row.

−	0	1	2	3	4	5	6	7	8	9
0	0	1	2	3	4	5	6	7	8	9
1	1	2	3	4	5	6	7	8	9	10
2	2	3	4	5	6	7	8	9	10	11
3	3	4	5	6	7	8	9	10	11	12
4	4	5	6	7	8	9	10	11	12	13
⑤	5	6	7	8	9	10	11	12	13	14
6	6	7	8	9	10	11	12	13	14	15
7	7	8	9	10	11	12	13	14	15	16
8	8	9	10	11	12	13	14	15	16	17
9	9	10	11	12	13	14	15	16	17	18

Subtract.

	a	b	c	d	e	f
1.	1 3 − 5	1 4 − 8	1 6 − 7	1 0 − 9	1 2 − 5	1 4 − 6
2.	1 7 − 8	1 3 − 7	1 2 − 4	1 4 − 5	1 5 − 8	1 3 − 6
3.	1 1 − 7	1 8 − 9	1 5 − 6	1 1 − 8	1 4 − 7	1 3 − 9
4.	1 6 − 8	1 0 − 5	1 2 − 7	1 3 − 4	1 2 − 6	1 4 − 9
5.	1 3 − 8	1 2 − 9	1 0 − 1	1 5 − 9	1 1 − 3	1 0 − 7
6.	1 5 − 7	1 0 − 3	1 7 − 9	1 1 − 6	1 6 − 9	1 1 − 4

Perfect score: 36   My score: _____

Problem Solving

Solve each problem.

1. Matt wants to collect 13 cars. He now has 5 cars. How many more cars does he need?

Matt wants _____ cars.

He now has _____ cars.

He needs _____ more cars.

2. Susan bought 18 valentines. She mailed 9 of them. How many valentines does she have left?

Susan bought _____ valentines.

She mailed _____ of them.

She has _____ valentines left.

3. Betty had 16 stamps. She used some, and had 7 left. How many stamps did she use?

Betty used _____ stamps.

4. Bret is 14 years old. Sally is 7. Bret is how much older than Sally?

Bret is _____ years older than Sally.

5. Fifteen bolts and nuts were on the table. Seven were bolts. How many were nuts?

There were _____ nuts.

6. There are 17 machine parts in a drawer. Only nine are new parts. How many are not new parts?

_____ are not new parts.

Perfect score: 10   My score: _____

14

Lesson 8   Addition and Subtraction

To check 6+8=14, subtract 8 from 14.	$\begin{array}{r} 6 \\ +8 \\ \hline 14 \\ -8 \\ \hline 6 \end{array}$	These should be the same.	

To check 13−6=7, add _____ to 7.	$\begin{array}{r} 13 \\ -6 \\ \hline 7 \\ +6 \\ \hline 13 \end{array}$	These should be the same.	

Add. Check each answer.

	a	b	c	d	e	f
1.	$\begin{array}{r} 5 \\ +9 \\ \hline \end{array}$	$\begin{array}{r} 9 \\ +7 \\ \hline \end{array}$	$\begin{array}{r} 6 \\ +6 \\ \hline \end{array}$	$\begin{array}{r} 7 \\ +4 \\ \hline \end{array}$	$\begin{array}{r} 9 \\ +8 \\ \hline \end{array}$	$\begin{array}{r} 3 \\ +7 \\ \hline \end{array}$
2.	$\begin{array}{r} 6 \\ +7 \\ \hline \end{array}$	$\begin{array}{r} 9 \\ +3 \\ \hline \end{array}$	$\begin{array}{r} 6 \\ +9 \\ \hline \end{array}$	$\begin{array}{r} 4 \\ +9 \\ \hline \end{array}$	$\begin{array}{r} 6 \\ +4 \\ \hline \end{array}$	$\begin{array}{r} 8 \\ +6 \\ \hline \end{array}$

Subtract. Check each answer.

3.	$\begin{array}{r} 14 \\ -8 \\ \hline \end{array}$	$\begin{array}{r} 18 \\ -9 \\ \hline \end{array}$	$\begin{array}{r} 13 \\ -5 \\ \hline \end{array}$	$\begin{array}{r} 15 \\ -6 \\ \hline \end{array}$	$\begin{array}{r} 16 \\ -8 \\ \hline \end{array}$	$\begin{array}{r} 12 \\ -7 \\ \hline \end{array}$
4.	$\begin{array}{r} 13 \\ -6 \\ \hline \end{array}$	$\begin{array}{r} 12 \\ -4 \\ \hline \end{array}$	$\begin{array}{r} 13 \\ -4 \\ \hline \end{array}$	$\begin{array}{r} 16 \\ -9 \\ \hline \end{array}$	$\begin{array}{r} 15 \\ -7 \\ \hline \end{array}$	$\begin{array}{r} 13 \\ -8 \\ \hline \end{array}$

Perfect score: 24   My score: _____

Problem Solving

Answer each question.

1. Penny worked 9 addition problems. She worked 7 subtraction problems. How many problems did she work?

Are you to add
  or subtract? _____

How many problems
  did she work? _____

2. Six people were in the room. Then 8 more people came in. How many people were in the room then?

Are you to add
  or subtract? _____

How many people were in the room then? _____

3. There were 18 chairs in a room. Nine of them were being used. How many were not being used?

Are you to add
  or subtract? _____

How many chairs
  were not being used? _____

4. Mr. Noe and Miss Leikel had 17 pupils absent. Mr. Noe had 9 absent. How many did Miss Leikel have absent?

Are you to add
  or subtract? _____

How many pupils were absent
  from Miss Leikel's class? _____

5. There were 14 children at the park. Five were boys. How many were girls?

Are you to add
  or subtract? _____

How many girls were at the park? _____

1.

2.

3.

4.

5.

Perfect score: 10   My score: _____

16

CHAPTER 1 TEST

Add.

	a	*b*	*c*	*d*	*e*	*f*
1.	7 +8	4 +9	6 +5	2 +8	8 +6	7 +5
2.	9 +1	5 +8	8 +4	9 +2	8 +8	5 +9
3.	5 +7	6 +9	8 +3	8 +9	3 +8	9 +4
4.	9 +6	6 +7	9 +9	6 +6	7 +9	6 +4
5.	8 +5	3 +9	1 +9	7 +4	3 +7	6 +8

Subtract.

	a	*b*	*c*	*d*	*e*
6.	1 0 − 6	1 4 − 7	1 2 − 3	1 5 − 7	1 2 − 8
7.	1 3 − 4	1 6 − 7	1 1 − 9	1 0 − 5	1 3 − 6
8.	1 0 − 2	1 4 − 6	1 1 − 6	1 2 − 7	1 7 − 9
9.	1 6 − 8	1 1 − 7	1 0 − 3	1 4 − 8	1 5 − 8

Perfect score: 50   My score: _____

PRE-TEST—Addition and Subtraction

Add.

	a	b	c	d	e	f
1.	3 +6	4 3 +6	1 +4	5 1 +4	2 +5	8 2 +5
2.	5 7 +2	2 6 +1	4 4 +3	2 3 +4	4 2 +3	2 1 +5
3.	4 +3 1	5 +4 3	4 +6 2	3 +4 3	5 +1 2	7 +2 0
4.	5 4 +3 1	2 6 +1 2	4 5 +3 3	6 7 +2 1	4 2 +3 3	2 2 +1 3
5.	3 2 +3 1	2 4 +2 4	3 6 +6 1	2 0 +1 9	4 5 +2 3	3 2 +2 1

Subtract.

	a	b	c	d	e	f
6.	7 −4	3 7 −4	5 −2	4 5 −2	8 −6	3 8 −6
7.	3 8 −4	2 7 −6	5 4 −3	2 9 −7	6 8 −2	2 6 −3
8.	5 4 −2 3	6 9 −2 4	3 7 −2 1	8 8 −2 4	9 3 −2 1	8 7 −3 7
9.	2 8 −1 3	5 4 −3 4	8 7 −2 6	5 4 −2 1	5 0 −4 0	3 7 −1 0

Perfect score: 54   My score: _____

18

Lesson 1 Addition

Add the ones.	Add the tens.		Add the ones.	Add the tens.
36 +2	36 +2 —— 8	36 +2 —— 38	6 +41	6 +41 —— 7	6 +41 —— 47

Add.

	a	b	c	d	e	f
1.	3 +5	2 3 +5	2 +3	4 2 +3	5 +1	2 5 +1
2.	3 +4	3 +6 4	4 +5	4 +5 5	2 +5	2 +8 5
3.	2 +4	1 2 +4	2 2 +4	3 2 +4	4 2 +4	5 2 +4
4.	5 +6 3	6 +3 1	2 4 +3	9 2 +2	5 7 +1	2 +4 1
5.	4 1 +3	2 1 +2	3 +6 3	2 +8 4	2 1 +6	4 +1 4
6.	8 +5 1	6 2 +4	2 5 +3	6 +3 3	2 +5 1	5 +4 3
7.	3 6 +2	4 2 +5	2 +5 1	6 0 +8	5 +2 1	3 4 +2

Perfect score: 42   My score: _____

19

Problem Solving

Solve each problem.

1. John has 32 red marbles and 5 green marbles. How many red and green marbles does he have?

John has _____ red and green marbles.

2. Su-Lee had 5 paper cups. She bought 24 more. How many paper cups did she have then?

She then had _____ paper cups.

3. On the way to work, Billy Joe counted 41 cars and 7 trucks. How many cars and trucks did he count?

Billy Joe counted _____ cars and trucks.

4. Mark worked all the problems on a test. He had 24 right answers and 4 wrong ones. How many problems were on the test?

There were _____ problems on the test.

5. Ruth works with 12 women and 6 men. How many people does she work with?

She works with _____ people.

6. Four men and 11 women are on the bus. How many people are on the bus?

_____ people are on the bus.

7. Marta weighs 20 kilograms. Her baby brother weighs 4 kilograms. How much do they weigh together?

They weigh _____ kilograms together.

1.

2.

3.

4.

5.

6.

7.

Perfect score: 7   My score: _____

20

Lesson 2   Addition

Add the ones.   Add the tens.

```
  36            36            36              25
+ 43          + 43          + 43            + 61
  ──            ──            ──              ──
               9             79              86
```

↑↑ —— Add the ones.
        —— Add the tens.

Add.

	a	b	c	d	e	f
1.	2 3 +4 5	6 3 +2 1	4 5 +2 2	6 1 +3 0	4 2 +3 5	6 0 +2 5
2.	4 8 +4 1	5 2 +1 4	3 2 +5 4	6 3 +2 0	2 1 +3 8	4 5 +5 2
3.	3 4 +2 2	4 1 +2 5	3 6 +2 2	5 1 +4 0	8 3 +1 2	4 2 +3 0
4.	6 3 +2 4	3 0 +5 8	2 7 +1 2	4 4 +2 3	6 2 +1 4	3 5 +5 3
5.	2 4 +3 1	5 2 +3 2	4 2 +2 7	5 1 +3 3	1 6 +2 0	4 3 +2 3
6.	3 4 +2 5	6 4 +2 3	1 8 +4 1	5 4 +2 4	4 1 +2 7	1 4 +3 2

Perfect score: 36   My score: _____

Problem Solving

Solve each problem.

1. There are 12 boys and 13 girls in Jean's class. How many pupils are in her class?

There are _____ pupils in that class.

2. Eve scored 32 baskets. She missed 23 times. How many times did she try to score?

Eve tried to score _____ times.

3. One store ordered 52 bicycles. Another store ordered 45 bicycles. How many bicycles did both stores order?

Both stores ordered _____ bicycles.

4. One bear cub weighs 64 kilograms. Another bear cub is 22 kilograms heavier. How much does the heavier cub weigh?

The heavier cub weighs _____ kilograms.

5. Johnny rode the bus 42 blocks east and 25 blocks south. How many blocks did Johnny ride the bus?

Johnny rode the bus _____ blocks.

6. 43 women and 35 men came to the meeting. How many people came to the meeting?

_____ people came to the meeting.

7. 68 seats were filled, and 21 were empty. How many seats were there?

There were _____ seats.

1.	
2.	3.
4.	5.
6.	7.

Perfect score: 7   My score: _____

22

Lesson 3   Subtraction

	Subtract the ones.	Subtract the tens.		Subtract the ones.	Subtract the tens.
47 −2	47 −2 5	47 −2 45	64 −23	64 −23 1	64 −23 41

Subtract.

	a	b	c	d	e	f
1.	9 −3	4 9 −3	5 −2	3 5 −2	7 −1	8 7 −1
2.	8 −2	7 8 −2	4 −3	6 4 −3	9 −9	8 9 −9
3.	4 5 −3	3 6 −4	7 8 −5	4 2 −2	3 8 −8	6 5 −4
4.	4 9 −2 6	3 7 −1 6	5 8 −2 3	4 9 −3 1	7 8 −4 5	7 3 −2 0
5.	5 8 −2 7	6 9 −3 1	4 2 −2 1	4 9 −1 9	8 4 −2 3	7 8 −6 4
6.	7 8 −2 1	6 7 −3 1	4 0 −2 0	5 6 −3 6	4 5 −2 3	9 2 −2 1
7.	5 6 −4 1	8 5 −6 3	9 4 −3 2	7 7 −4 6	9 9 −3 2	8 6 −2 3

Perfect score: 42   My score: _____

Problem Solving

Solve each problem.

1. Beth worked 27 problems. She got 6 wrong answers. How many answers did she get right?

Beth got _____ answers right.

2. There were 96 parts in a box. Four parts were broken. How many parts were not broken?

_____ parts were not broken.

3. At noon the temperature was 28 degrees Celsius. At nine o'clock in the evening it was 14 degrees Celsius. How many degrees did the temperature drop?

The temperature dropped _____ degrees.

4. Clark had 75 cents. Then he spent 25 cents for some paper. How many cents did he have left?

Clark had _____ cents left.

5. There are 72 houses in Fred's neighborhood. Fred delivers papers to all but 21 of them. How many houses does he deliver papers to?

He delivers papers to _____ houses.

6. Ninety-five pupils were in the gym. Thirty-four were boys. How many were girls?

_____ pupils were girls.

7. A rope is 47 inches long. A wire is 17 inches long. How much longer is the rope?

The rope is _____ inches longer.

1.	
2.	3.
4.	5.
6.	7.

Perfect score: 7   My score: _____

Lesson 4   Subtraction

To check	37
37 − 24 = 13,	− 24
add 24	———
to _____.	13
	+ 24
	———
	37

These should be the same.

To check	59
59 − 29 = 30,	− 29
	———
add _____	30
to 30.	+ 29
	———
	59

These should be the same.

Subtract. Check each answer.

	a	b	c	d	e	f
1.	59 −34	27 −14	85 −23	78 −23	47 −24	59 −26
2.	85 −25	48 −32	56 −24	96 −35	40 −30	92 −81
3.	74 −23	58 −26	75 −24	38 −23	45 −35	88 −35
4.	67 −24	87 −24	59 −36	58 −24	79 −54	84 −23

Perfect score: 24   My score: _____

Problem Solving

Solve each problem.

1. Mr. Ming wants to build a fence 58 meters long. He has 27 meters of fence completed. How much of the fence is left to build?

_____ meters of fence is left to build.

2. Mr. Boyle is taking an 89-mile trip. He has traveled 64 miles. How much farther must he travel?

Mr. Boyle must travel _____ more miles.

3. Sean had 95 cents. Then he spent 45 cents. How many cents did he have left?

Sean had _____ cents left.

4. Beverly scored 62 points and Dorothy scored 78 points. How many more points did Dorothy score than Beverly?

Dorothy scored _____ more points.

5. Bill lives 38 blocks from the ball park. Joe lives 25 blocks from the park. How much farther from the ball park does Bill live than Joe?

Bill lives _____ blocks farther than Joe.

6. Eighty-four pupils were in the pool. Fifty of them were boys. How many girls were in the pool?

_____ girls were in the pool.

7. Larry said that 88 buses stop at Division Street each day. So far, 13 buses have stopped. How many more buses should stop today?

_____ more buses should stop.

1.

2.

3.

4.

5.

6.

7.

Perfect score: 7   My score: _____

Lesson 5   Addition and Subtraction

To check
$43 + 14 = 57$,
subtract 14
from _____.

$$\begin{array}{r} 43 \\ +14 \\ \hline 57 \\ -14 \\ \hline 43 \end{array}$$

These should
be the same.

To check
$57 - 14 = 43$,

add _____
to 43.

$$\begin{array}{r} 57 \\ -14 \\ \hline 43 \\ +14 \\ \hline 57 \end{array}$$

These should
be the same.

Add. Check each answer.

	a	*b*	*c*	*d*	*e*	*f*
1.	27 +31	42 +51	26 +30	14 +52	23 +72	65 +22
2.	44 +24	31 +27	64 +14	32 +20	42 +36	46 +23

Subtract. Check each answer.

	a	*b*	*c*	*d*	*e*	*f*
3.	78 −23	48 −13	27 −16	58 −26	67 −24	38 −16
4.	75 −61	46 −26	39 −10	45 −23	67 −41	38 −15

Perfect score: 24   My score: _____

Problem Solving

Solve each problem.

1. Mrs. Dial weighs 55 kilograms. Her son weighs 32 kilograms. How much more thar her son does Mrs. Dial weigh?

She weighs _____ kilograms more.

2. Mitzi planted 55 flower seeds. Only 23 of them grew. How many did not grow?

_____ seeds did not grow.

3. A city has 48 mail trucks. Twelve are not being used today. How many mail trucks are being used?

_____ mail trucks are being used.

4. A mail carrier delivered 38 letters and picked up 15. How many more letters were delivered than were picked up?

The carrier delivered _____ more letters.

5. A city has 89 mail carriers. One day 77 carriers were at work. How many were not at work?

_____ carriers were not at work.

6. Our mail carrier walks about 32 miles each week. About how many miles does our carrier walk in two weeks?

Our carrier walks _____ miles in two weeks.

7. Ms. Tottle worked at a store for 23 years. She then worked 26 years at a bank. How many years did she work at these two places?

She worked _____ years at these two places.

1.	
2.	**3.**
4.	**5.**
6.	**7.**

Perfect score: 7   My score: _____

28

CHAPTER 2 TEST

Add or subtract. Check each answer.

	a	*b*	*c*	*d*	*e*	*f*
1.	4 +2	2 4 +2	3 6 +3	4 +2 1	7 2 +4	9 +3 0
2.	3 6 +2 1	4 1 +3 8	6 5 +2 2	4 1 +2 6	3 5 +5 0	6 6 +2 1
3.	7 −2	3 7 −2	4 5 −4	2 6 −3	4 9 −8	2 7 −5
4.	4 8 −2 3	6 5 −2 4	4 5 −2 2	6 8 −2 8	5 4 −2 2	6 7 −3 0

Solve.

5. Miss Jones has 32 pupils. Mr. Lum has 26 pupils.
How many pupils are in the two classes?

There are _____ pupils in the two classes.

Perfect score: 25   My score: _____

PRE-TEST—Addition and Subtraction

Add.

	a	*b*	*c*	*d*	*e*	*f*
1.	5 3 +6	2 4 +2	2 +3 5	8 +8 1	6 4 +3	2 5 +2
2.	3 6 +5	5 4 +8	8 +3 9	2 +5 9	4 8 +8	2 6 +7
3.	4 2 +3 3	7 2 +1 4	5 4 +2 3	6 1 +2 8	1 9 +4 0	2 6 +5 2
4.	5 4 +2 7	3 5 +3 6	5 9 +3 8	5 4 +1 9	2 7 +4 8	3 9 +3 9
5.	4 9 +2 3	6 2 +1 7	4 3 +2 1	4 8 +4 8	2 6 +4 0	5 6 +3 7

Subtract.

	a	*b*	*c*	*d*	*e*	*f*
6.	3 7 −3	2 9 −4	5 4 −4	8 7 −2	5 6 −5	8 9 −6
7.	4 7 −9	7 2 −5	4 5 −7	5 5 −9	4 0 −5	3 4 −7
8.	5 4 −1 2	4 2 −3 0	7 5 −6 4	4 6 −2 3	9 3 −8 1	8 9 −4 1
9.	7 3 −2 5	8 5 −4 9	9 2 −2 4	6 4 −5 6	7 7 −4 8	8 8 −3 8

Perfect score: 54   My score: _____

Lesson 1 Addition

Add the ones.
Rename 13 as 10 + 3.

Add the tens.

$$54 \atop +9$$

$$4 \atop +9 \over 13 \text{ or } 10+3$$

$$\overset{1}{5}4 \atop +9 \over 3$$

$$\overset{1}{5}4 \atop +9 \over 63$$

Add.

	a	b	c	d	e	f
1.	27 +5	35 +8	87 +4	38 +9	42 +8	46 +5
2.	45 +9	27 +7	7 +38	20 +65	24 +9	8 +38
3.	27 +3	45 +6	8 +36	9 +29	6 +58	42 +9
4.	76 +7	3 +47	4 +26	27 +4	5 +18	9 +19
5.	6 +15	41 +9	52 +8	65 +9	7 +38	6 +16
6.	9 +28	36 +7	59 +2	7 +36	4 +47	9 +38
7.	46 +8	9 +25	8 +68	4 +59	85 +5	78 +7

Perfect score: 42   My score: _____

Problem Solving

Solve each problem.

1. Last year there were 44 monkeys on an island. There are 8 more monkeys this year. How many monkeys are on the island now?

There were _____ monkeys last year.

There are _____ more monkeys this year.

There are _____ monkeys on the island now.

2. There were 72 children and 9 adults in our group at the zoo. How many people were in our group?

_____ children were in our group.

_____ adults were in our group.

_____ people were in our group.

3. One group of monkeys was fed 6 kilograms of fruit. Another group was fed 19 kilograms. How much fruit was that in all?

That was _____ kilograms of fruit in all.

4. The children drank 68 cartons of milk. There were 8 cartons left. How many cartons of milk were there to start with?

There were _____ cartons of milk to start with.

5. A zoo has 87 kinds of snakes. They are getting 4 new kinds. How many kinds will they have then?

Then they will have _____ kinds of snakes.

1.

2.

3.

4.   5.

Perfect score: 9   My score: _____

32

Lesson 2   Addition

Add the ones.
Rename 15 as 10 + 5.

Add the tens.

```
  48
+ 27
-----
```

```
  8          4̅8          ⁱ4̅8
+ 7        + 27        + 27
-----      -----       -----
15 or 10 + 5   5          75
```

Add.

	a	b	c	d	e	f
1.	37 +25	48 +37	26 +54	35 +29	54 +18	62 +29
2.	29 +28	38 +37	47 +25	63 +27	79 +19	64 +17
3.	58 +26	45 +18	27 +57	44 +29	36 +36	77 +17
4.	49 +48	26 +37	73 +19	18 +28	15 +47	29 +27
5.	18 +55	28 +24	38 +37	48 +43	58 +16	68 +28
6.	26 +66	19 +54	57 +29	45 +36	52 +18	33 +29
7.	35 +56	47 +28	31 +39	29 +59	67 +16	55 +28

Perfect score: 42   My score: _____

33

Problem Solving

Solve each problem.

1. January has 31 days. February has 29 days this year. How many days are in the two months?

There are _____ days in January.

There are _____ days in February this year.

There are _____ days in January and February.

2. Jeff weighs 46 kilograms. His father is 36 kilograms heavier. How much does Jeff's father weigh?

Jeff weighs _____ kilograms.

His father is _____ kilograms heavier.

His father weighs _____ kilograms.

3. Mary had 29 points. She earned 13 more. How many points did she have then?

Mary had _____ points.

She earned _____ more.

She had _____ points then.

4. Hank gained 18 pounds in the last two years. Two years ago he weighed 59 pounds. How much does he weigh today?

Hank weighs _____ pounds today.

5. Kathy read 25 pages of a story. She has 36 more pages to read. How many pages are there in the story?

There are _____ pages in the story.

1.

2.

3.

4.

5.

Perfect score: 11   My score: _____

Lesson 3 Subtraction

To subtract the ones, rename 63 as "5 tens and 13 ones."

Subtract the ones.

Subtract the tens.

$$\begin{array}{r} 63 \\ -9 \\ \hline \end{array}$$

$$\begin{array}{r} ^{5}\cancel{6}\ ^{13}\cancel{3} \\ -9 \\ \hline \end{array}$$

$$\begin{array}{r} ^{5}\cancel{6}\ ^{13}\cancel{3} \\ -9 \\ \hline 4 \end{array}$$

$$\begin{array}{r} ^{5}\cancel{6}\ ^{13}\cancel{3} \\ -9 \\ \hline 5\ 4 \end{array}$$

Subtract.

	a	b	c	d	e	f
1.	53 −8	27 −9	46 −9	54 −5	32 −6	65 −7
2.	28 −9	48 −9	35 −6	44 −7	67 −8	92 −9
3.	52 −6	62 −4	61 −6	73 −5	50 −9	42 −5
4.	96 −8	73 −6	80 −7	42 −3	63 −4	51 −9
5.	94 −8	88 −9	33 −4	27 −9	46 −8	64 −7
6.	23 −9	76 −8	40 −4	41 −6	53 −7	25 −7
7.	47 −8	31 −7	82 −8	74 −6	93 −9	60 −5

Perfect score: 42   My score: _____

Problem Solving

Solve each problem.

1. There were 48 words on a spelling test. Sarah missed 9 of them. How many words did she spell correctly?

There were _____ words on the test.

Sarah missed _____ words.

She spelled _____ words correctly.

2. Frank earned 91 points. Mike earned 5 points less than Frank. How many points did Mike earn?

Frank earned _____ points.

Mike earned _____ points less than Frank.

Mike earned _____ points.

3. Sheila lost 7 of the 45 games she played. How many games did she win?

She won _____ games.

4. Ken had 50 tickets to sell. He sold some and had 6 left. How many tickets did he sell?

Ken sold _____ tickets.

5. There were 73 books in the classroom library. Some of the books are checked out. Seven are still there. How many books are checked out?

_____ books are checked out.

6. Angela's great-grandfather is 82 years old. How old was he 4 years ago?

Four years ago he was _____ years old.

1.	
2.	
3.	**4.**
5.	**6.**

Perfect score: 10   My score: _____

Lesson 4 Subtraction

To subtract the ones, rename 92 as "8 tens and 12 ones."

Subtract the ones.

Subtract the tens.

$$
\begin{array}{r} 92 \\ -38 \\ \hline \end{array}
\qquad
\begin{array}{r} \overset{8}{\cancel{9}}\,\overset{12}{\cancel{2}} \\ -3\ 8 \\ \hline \end{array}
\qquad
\begin{array}{r} \overset{8}{\cancel{9}}\,\overset{12}{\cancel{2}} \\ -3\ 8 \\ \hline 4 \end{array}
\qquad
\begin{array}{r} \overset{8}{\cancel{9}}\,\overset{12}{\cancel{2}} \\ -3\ 8 \\ \hline 5\ 4 \end{array}
$$

Subtract.

	a	b	c	d	e	f
1.	35 −17	27 −19	54 −37	63 −26	84 −59	28 −19
2.	42 −24	56 −39	41 −27	53 −15	86 −78	92 −26
3.	43 −15	37 −29	26 −19	55 −36	43 −27	28 −19
4.	54 −26	35 −18	22 −15	56 −29	38 −19	31 −18
5.	83 −25	94 −16	65 −39	73 −17	80 −28	92 −35
6.	35 −26	90 −55	56 −27	41 −16	50 −38	61 −15
7.	52 −18	75 −38	47 −39	60 −11	86 −59	94 −48

Perfect score: 42   My score: _____

37

Problem Solving

Solve each problem.

1. Joe weighs 95 pounds. Larry weighs 26 pounds less than Joe. How much does Larry weigh?

Joe weighs _____ pounds.

Larry weighs _____ pounds less than Joe.

Larry weighs _____ pounds.

2. There are 73 children in the gym. Forty-five of them are boys. How many girls are in the gym?

There are _____ children in the gym.

There are _____ boys in the gym.

There are _____ girls in the gym.

3. A store has 84 bicycles. They have 45 girls' bicycles. How many boys' bicycles do they have?

_____ bicycles are boy's bicycles.

4. It takes 50 points to win a prize. Penny has 38 points. How many more points does Penny need to win a prize?

Penny needs _____ points.

5. Ann has 19 more pages to read in a book. The book has 46 pages in all. How many pages has Ann already read?

Ann has already read _____ pages.

6. The Tigers scored 33 points. The Bears scored 18 points. How many more points did the Tigers score than the Bears?

The Tigers scored _____ more points.

1.

2.

3.

4.

5.

6.

Perfect score: 10   My score: _____

38

Lesson 5   Addition and Subtraction

To check
$34 + 19 = 53$,
subtract 19
from _____ .

$$\begin{array}{r} 34 \\ +19 \\ \hline 53 \\ -19 \\ \hline 34 \end{array}$$

These should
be the same.

To check
$53 - 19 = 34$,

add _____
to 34.

$$\begin{array}{r} 53 \\ -19 \\ \hline 34 \\ +19 \\ \hline 53 \end{array}$$

These should
be the same.

Add. Check each answer.

	a	*b*	*c*	*d*	*e*	*f*
1.	$\begin{array}{r} 54 \\ +7 \\ \hline \end{array}$	$\begin{array}{r} 46 \\ +9 \\ \hline \end{array}$	$\begin{array}{r} 63 \\ +18 \\ \hline \end{array}$	$\begin{array}{r} 58 \\ +27 \\ \hline \end{array}$	$\begin{array}{r} 21 \\ +49 \\ \hline \end{array}$	$\begin{array}{r} 45 \\ +46 \\ \hline \end{array}$
2.	$\begin{array}{r} 26 \\ +38 \\ \hline \end{array}$	$\begin{array}{r} 37 \\ +19 \\ \hline \end{array}$	$\begin{array}{r} 41 \\ +9 \\ \hline \end{array}$	$\begin{array}{r} 58 \\ +18 \\ \hline \end{array}$	$\begin{array}{r} 67 \\ +27 \\ \hline \end{array}$	$\begin{array}{r} 35 \\ +38 \\ \hline \end{array}$

Subtract. Check each answer.

3.	$\begin{array}{r} 62 \\ -8 \\ \hline \end{array}$	$\begin{array}{r} 48 \\ -9 \\ \hline \end{array}$	$\begin{array}{r} 35 \\ -16 \\ \hline \end{array}$	$\begin{array}{r} 96 \\ -29 \\ \hline \end{array}$	$\begin{array}{r} 52 \\ -14 \\ \hline \end{array}$	$\begin{array}{r} 43 \\ -5 \\ \hline \end{array}$
4.	$\begin{array}{r} 36 \\ -18 \\ \hline \end{array}$	$\begin{array}{r} 57 \\ -8 \\ \hline \end{array}$	$\begin{array}{r} 67 \\ -19 \\ \hline \end{array}$	$\begin{array}{r} 52 \\ -17 \\ \hline \end{array}$	$\begin{array}{r} 51 \\ -23 \\ \hline \end{array}$	$\begin{array}{r} 60 \\ -46 \\ \hline \end{array}$

Perfect score: 24   My score: _____

Problem Solving

Answer each question.

1. This morning the temperature was 75 degrees. This afternoon it was 83 degrees. How many degrees did it go up?

Are you to add
or subtract? _____

How many degrees did
the temperature go up? _____

1.

2. There were 45 people at a meeting. After 28 of them left, how many people were still at the meeting?

Are you to add
or subtract? _____

How many people
were still at the meeting? _____

2.

3. Renée drove 67 miles in the morning and 24 miles in the afternoon. How far did she drive?

Are you to add
or subtract? _____

How far did she drive? _____

3.

4. Harry is 54 inches tall. His sister is 36 inches tall. How much taller is Harry?

Are you to add
or subtract? _____

How much taller is
Harry than his sister? _____

4.

5. A clown has 26 orange balloons and 28 blue balloons. How many balloons is that?

Are you to add
or subtract? _____

How many orange and
blue balloons are there? _____

5.

Perfect score: 10   My score: _____

40

CHAPTER 3 TEST

Add. Check each answer.

	a	b	c	d	e	f
1.	3 6 +7	4 5 +9	8 +2 3	1 7 +7	8 +4 4	5 8 +6

2.	1 7 +2 5	2 6 +4 8	4 3 +3 8	7 4 +1 9	7 8 +1 8	6 5 +1 6

Subtract. Check each answer.

3.	2 6 −8	5 4 −9	6 1 −3	2 7 −9	5 4 −6	6 6 −9

4.	3 6 −1 7	7 2 −4 4	3 8 −1 9	7 4 −2 6	9 3 −8 9	8 2 −5 7

Solve.

5. Fifty-four girls and 27 boys came to the meeting.
How many boys and girls came to the meeting?

_____ boys and girls came to the meeting.

Perfect score: 25   My score: _____

41

PRE-TEST—Addition and Subtraction

Add.

	a	b	c	d	e	f
1.	5 +6	5 0 +6 0	7 +8	7 0 +8 0	9 0 +8 0	7 0 +7 0
2.	5 3 +9 5	4 4 +7 4	8 2 +9 6	6 7 +7 0	5 5 +5 2	7 3 +8 6
3.	6 3 +7 8	8 2 +8 9	9 7 +2 7	5 6 +7 5	8 8 +8 8	9 7 +4 4
4.	2 6 +5 3	6 6 +2 5	7 4 +6 5	3 9 +8 7	8 2 +1 7	7 6 +7 2
5.	5 9 +5 9	7 3 +1 5	8 3 +6 7	5 4 +7 2	6 3 +7 0	3 5 +4 5

Subtract.

	a	b	c	d	e	f
6.	1 6 −7	1 6 0 −7 0	1 5 −9	1 5 0 −9 0	1 4 0 −6 0	1 7 0 −8 0
7.	1 3 6 −5 3	1 6 5 −7 4	1 5 4 −9 0	1 8 6 −9 3	1 7 9 −8 2	1 4 7 −6 7
8.	1 4 6 −9 7	1 5 8 −6 9	1 7 2 −8 5	1 6 3 −7 7	1 2 5 −5 8	1 1 6 −3 9
9.	1 7 6 −5 3	1 8 4 −3 5	1 5 4 −7 2	1 5 3 −7 4	1 4 6 −3 2	1 0 7 −4 0

Perfect score: 54   My score: _____

Lesson 1 Addition and Subtraction

8	8	80	80	14	14	140	140
+6	+6	+60	+60	−6	−6	−60	−60
	14		140		8		80

If 8 + 6 = 14, then 80 + 60 = _____.   If 14 − 6 = 8, then 140 − 60 = _____.

Add.

	a	b	c	d	e	f
1.	7 +8	7 0 +8 0	6 +9	6 0 +9 0	3 +8	3 0 +8 0
2.	7 +5	7 0 +5 0	8 +9	8 0 +9 0	4 +6	4 0 +6 0
3.	7 0 +4 0	5 0 +9 0	3 0 +9 0	7 0 +7 0	9 0 +4 0	8 0 +4 0
4.	2 0 +9 0	6 0 +6 0	7 0 +6 0	9 0 +1 0	7 0 +9 0	8 0 +8 0

Subtract.

	a	b	c	d	e	f
5.	1 3 −5	1 3 0 −5 0	1 7 −8	1 7 0 −8 0	1 2 −6	1 2 0 −6 0
6.	1 5 −6	1 5 0 −6 0	1 4 −5	1 4 0 −5 0	1 8 −9	1 8 0 −9 0
7.	1 4 0 −8 0	1 1 0 −7 0	1 6 0 −8 0	1 3 0 −6 0	1 7 0 −9 0	1 2 0 −5 0
8.	1 3 0 −9 0	1 6 0 −7 0	1 5 0 −8 0	1 2 0 −8 0	1 4 0 −9 0	1 1 0 −4 0

Perfect score: 48   My score: _____

Problem Solving

Answer each question.

1. Harold is on a trip of 170 kilometers. So far he has gone 90 kilometers. How many more kilometers must he go?

Are you to add
or subtract? _____

How many more
kilometers must he go? _____

2. A school has 60 men teachers. It has 60 women teachers. How many teachers are in the school?

Are you to add
or subtract? _____

How many teachers are in the school? _____

3. Ken weighs 70 pounds. His older brother weighs 130 pounds. How many more pounds does his older brother weigh?

Are you to add
or subtract? _____

How many more pounds does
his older brother weigh? _____

4. Joyce has 110 pennies. Emily has 90 pennies. Joyce has how many more pennies than Emily?

Joyce has _____ more pennies than Emily.

5. Vera sold 50 pennants on Monday and 70 on Tuesday. How many pennants did she sell in all?

Vera sold _____ pennants in all.

6. A bag contains 150 red and green marbles. Ninety of them are red. How many marbles are green?

_____ marbles are green.

1.

2.

3.	4.

5.	6.

Perfect score: 9   My score: _____

44

Lesson 2   Addition

Add the ones.   Add the tens.

```
   43            43                    43
  +86           +86                   +86
               ___                   ____
                 9                   129
                 ↑                    ↑ ↑
            3 + 6 = 9      40 + 80 = 120 or 100 + 20
```

Add.

	a	b	c	d	e	f

1.
   74   56   49   57   83   94
  +62   +93   +60   +72   +35   +24

2.
   62   76   34   83   96   72
  +53   +72   +95   +43   +61   +41

3.
   92   74   93   86   55   34
  +30   +82   +92   +21   +60   +82

4.
   65   54   83   46   93   62
  +42   +82   +93   +90   +93   +64

5.
   81   65   42   35   90   80
  +58   +91   +84   +72   +70   +85

6.
   93   22   45   54   43   61
  +84   +97   +72   +54   +82   +81

7.
   56   62   70   54   94   85
  +82   +43   +76   +73   +94   +92

Perfect score: 42   My score: _____

Problem Solving

Solve each problem.

1. Richard sold 96 tickets. Carmen sold 81. How many tickets did they both sell?

Richard sold _____ tickets.

Carmen sold _____ tickets.

They sold a total of _____ tickets.

2. Fifty-three people live in the first building. Eighty-five people live in the second building. How many people live in both buildings?

_____ people live in the first building.

_____ people live in the second building.

_____ people live in both buildings.

3. A train went 83 kilometers the first hour. The second hour it went 84 kilometers. How far did it go in the two hours?

The first hour
   the train went _____ kilometers.

The second
   hour it went _____ kilometers.

In the two
   hours it went _____ kilometers.

4. Ninety-two train seats are filled. There are 47 empty train seats. How many train seats are there?

There are _____ train seats.

5. Joy collected 72 stamps. Jan collected 76 stamps. How many stamps did they collect in all?

They collected _____ stamps.

1.

2.

3.

4.

5.

Perfect score: 11   My score: _____

46

Lesson 3 Subtraction

	Subtract the ones.	To subtract the tens, rename 1 hundred and 3 tens as "13 tens."	Subtract the tens.

$$
\begin{array}{r} 136 \\ -72 \\ \hline \end{array}
\qquad
\begin{array}{r} 136 \\ -72 \\ \hline 4 \end{array}
\qquad
\begin{array}{r} \overset{13}{136} \\ -72 \\ \hline 4 \end{array}
\qquad
\begin{array}{r} \overset{13}{1\!\!\!/36} \\ -72 \\ \hline 64 \end{array}
$$

Subtract.

	a	b	c	d	e	f
1.	147 −64	108 −72	156 −83	129 −44	175 −81	114 −42
2.	136 −86	153 −62	118 −91	124 −82	136 −43	107 −45
3.	148 −82	164 −83	186 −93	115 −72	104 −91	146 −52
4.	107 −23	139 −72	124 −3.0	155 −95	166 −72	124 −61
5.	118 −27	126 −55	174 −93	149 −72	108 −61	136 −94
6.	145 −92	129 −73	152 −72	164 −90	135 −62	113 −61
7.	126 −91	185 −94	137 −65	158 −86	149 −99	176 −83

Perfect score: 42   My score: _____

Problem Solving

Solve each problem.

1. Bob had 128 centimeters of string. He used 73 centimeters of it. How much string was left?

The string was _____ centimeters long.

Bob used _____ centimeters of the string.

There were _____ centimeters of string left.

2. Francis and Diane got on a scale. The reading was "145 pounds." Diane got off, and the reading was "75 pounds." How much does Diane weigh?

Together they weighed _____ pounds.

Francis weighs _____ pounds.

Diane weighs _____ pounds.

3. There are 167 pupils in Tony's grade at school. Seventy-one of the pupils are girls. How many of the pupils are boys?

There are _____ pupils in all.

There are _____ girls.

There are _____ boys.

4. Judy counted 156 sheets of paper in the package. Then she used 91 sheets. How many sheets of paper did she have left?

There were _____ sheets of paper left.

5. A jet plane has 184 passenger seats. There are 93 passengers on the plane. How many empty passenger seats are there?

There are _____ empty passenger seats.

1.

2.

3.

4.	5.

Perfect score: 11   My score: _____

48

Lesson 4 Addition and Subtraction

To check
75 + 61 = 136,
subtract _____
from 136.

$$\begin{array}{r} 75 \\ +61 \\ \hline 136 \\ -61 \\ \hline 75 \end{array}$$

These should
be the same.

To check
157 − 83 = 74,
add 83
to _____.

$$\begin{array}{r} 157 \\ -83 \\ \hline 74 \\ +83 \\ \hline 157 \end{array}$$

These should
be the same.

Add. Check each answer.

	a	b	c	d	e	f
1.	74 +53	85 +42	96 +60	43 +71	61 +45	32 +82
2.	91 +82	53 +63	96 +51	45 +82	32 +96	53 +51

Subtract. Check each answer.

3.	175 −83	156 −64	162 −91	189 −95	144 −60	128 −71
4.	136 −62	165 −83	157 −76	128 −61	147 −52	104 −21

Perfect score: 24   My score: _____

Problem Solving

Solve each problem.

1. Derrick worked at the computer for 80 minutes in the morning. That afternoon he worked at it for 40 minutes. How long did he work on the computer that day?

Are you to add or subtract? _____

How long did he work on
the computer that day? _____

1.

2. Derrick wrote a computer program that has 129 lines. He has put 91 lines in the computer so far. How many more lines does he have to put in the computer?

Are you to add or subtract? _____

How many more lines does
he have to put in the computer? _____

2.

3. Derrick's mother uses the computer for work. Last month she used it 71 hours. This month she used it for 82 hours. How many hours did she use the computer in the last two months?

Are you to add or subtract? _____

How many hours did she use the
computer in the last two months? _____

3.

Perfect score: 6   My score: _____

Lesson 5 Addition

Add the ones.   Add the tens.

$$
\begin{array}{r} 58 \\ +76 \\ \hline \end{array}
\qquad
\begin{array}{r} \overset{1}{5}8 \\ +76 \\ \hline 4 \end{array}
\qquad
\begin{array}{r} \overset{1}{5}8 \\ +76 \\ \hline 134 \end{array}
$$

$8+6=14$ or $10+4$ $10+50+70=130$ or $100+30$

Add.

	a	b	c	d	e	f
1.	94 +68	77 +46	59 +75	72 +38	43 +99	66 +85
2.	87 +85	39 +92	66 +46	47 +78	75 +55	89 +96
3.	97 +59	89 +59	16 +95	34 +88	63 +98	99 +48
4.	37 +73	94 +28	99 +32	58 +95	67 +75	29 +85
5.	48 +86	69 +57	94 +97	72 +88	89 +64	87 +26
6.	54 +88	76 +76	89 +98	43 +68	96 +29	78 +68

Perfect score: 36   My score: _____

Problem Solving

Solve each problem.

1. A library loaned 74 books on Monday. It loaned 87 books on Tuesday. How many books did it loan on both days?

The library loaned _____ books on Monday.

The library loaned _____ books on Tuesday.

The library loaned _____ books both days.

2. Barbara read 49 pages in the morning. She read 57 pages in the afternoon. How many pages did she read in all?

Barbara read _____ pages in the morning.

Barbara read _____ pages in the afternoon.

Barbara read _____ pages in all.

3. The gym is 48 feet longer than the basketball court. The basketball court is 84 feet long. How long is the gym?

The basketball court is _____ feet long.

The gym is _____ feet longer
    than the basketball court.

The gym is _____ feet long.

4. At the circus, 84 adult tickets and 96 children's tickets were sold. How many tickets were sold?

_____ tickets were sold.

5. The team scored 66 points in the first half. They scored 68 points the second half. How many points did they score in the game?

They scored _____ points in the game.

1.
2.
3.

4.	5.

Perfect score: 11   My score: _____

Lesson 6   Subtraction

Rename 1 hundred and 6 ones as "10 tens and 6 ones."

Rename 10 tens and 6 ones as "9 tens and 16 ones."

Subtract the ones.

Subtract the tens.

```
  106        106         106         106         106
 - 49       - 49        - 49        - 49        - 49
                                      7          57
```

Subtract.

	a	b	c	d	e	f
1.	135 −86	108 −19	113 −27	125 −48	142 −59	156 −88
2.	115 −78	122 −78	171 −99	140 −55	107 −18	132 −65
3.	186 −99	153 −65	132 −93	148 −79	115 −57	142 −64
4.	153 −95	104 −37	136 −48	150 −77	162 −95	174 −86
5.	143 −85	154 −96	163 −87	132 −75	120 −61	147 −78
6.	163 −99	174 −87	126 −58	142 −95	133 −58	114 −28
7.	102 −23	175 −97	166 −97	148 −59	133 −74	121 −98

Perfect score: 42   My score: _____

Problem Solving

Solve each problem.

1. Ms. Davis needs 180 meters of fence. She has 95 meters of fence. How many more meters of fence does she need?

Ms. Davis needs _____ meters of fence.

She has _____ meters of fence.

She needs _____ more meters of fence.

2. Eddie knows the names of 128 pupils at school. If 79 are girls, how many are boys?

Eddie knows the names of _____ pupils.

_____ are girls.

_____ are boys.

3. Margo's family is on a 162-kilometer trip. They have already gone 84 kilometers. How much farther do they have to go?

The trip is _____ kilometers long.

They have gone _____ kilometers.

They have _____ more kilometers to go.

4. Ted's birthday is the 29th day of the year. Karen's birthday is the 126th day. Karen's birthday is how many days after Ted's birthday?

It is _____ days after Ted's birthday?

5. Mr. Darter got 131 trading stamps at two stores. He got 84 stamps at one store. How many did he get at the other store?

Mr. Darter got _____ stamps.

1.

2.

3.

4.   5.

Perfect score: 11   My score: _____

54

Lesson 7   Addition and Subtraction

Add. Check each answer.

	a	b	c	d	e	f
1.	5 4 +3 8	7 1 +5 6	5 7 +8 6	9 5 +2 4	4 2 +3 7	5 8 +2 6
2.	7 2 +9 6	5 8 +7 4	9 2 +3 7	4 8 +2 2	3 5 +4 3	5 5 +5 5

Subtract. Check each answer.

	a	b	c	d	e	f
3.	1 2 5 −9 2	1 7 4 −3 3	1 6 5 −8 7	1 5 0 −9 0	1 4 6 −7 6	1 3 2 −8 4
4.	1 1 2 −4 7	1 1 8 −3 3	1 5 7 −2 6	1 6 0 −4 5	1 7 5 −7 6	1 5 3 −8 3
5.	1 9 8 −3 9	1 5 5 −9 7	1 6 3 −8 4	1 3 1 −7 1	1 1 1 −2 4	1 0 8 −3 9

Perfect score: 30   My score: _____

Problem Solving

Solve each problem.

1. There are 166 people living in my apartment building. If 98 are children, how many are adults?

There are _____ people in the building.

There are _____ children.

There are _____ adults.

2. There were 115 cases on a truck. The driver left 27 cases at the first stop. How many cases are still on the truck?

_____ cases were on a truck.

_____ cases were left at the first stop.

_____ cases are still on the truck.

3. The bus has 84 passenger seats. All the seats are filled and there are 39 passengers standing. How many passengers are on the bus?

The bus has _____ seats.

There are _____ passengers standing.

There are _____ passengers on the bus.

4. Beth counted 63 houses on one side of the street. She counted 89 on the other side. How many houses are on the street?

There are _____ houses on the street.

5. Martha had 112 balloons. She gave some of them away. She had 35 balloons left. How many balloons did she give away?

She gave away _____ balloons.

1.

2.

3.

4.

5.

Perfect score: 11   My score: _____

56

CHAPTER 4 TEST

Add or subtract. Check each answer.

	a	b	c	d	e
1.	6 0 +8 0	7 0 +9 0	8 5 +6 3	7 2 +5 4	6 0 +6 5
2.	8 4 +5 7	6 3 +7 7	8 2 +9 9	7 8 +7 8	4 4 +7 9
3.	1 7 0 −8 0	1 6 0 −8 0	1 5 3 −7 1	1 2 7 −8 2	1 7 5 −9 1
4.	1 2 7 −5 9	1 4 3 −6 5	1 6 6 −8 9	1 8 3 −9 5	1 2 2 −5 7
5.	1 4 7 −3 6	5 6 +3 7	1 7 5 −8 5	5 7 +8 9	1 9 7 −7 3

Perfect score: 25   My score: _____

PRE-TEST—Addition and Subtraction

Add.

	a	*b*	*c*	*d*	*e*	*f*
1.	3 4 +7	8 6 +9	9 5 +7	5 6 8 +3	4 9 2 +6	3 7 5 +9
2.	10 30 40 +50	20 30 40 +60	20 40 60 +70	40 30 80 +40	50 50 20 +60	20 60 20 +40
3.	52 41 +30	26 30 +92	33 44 +57	38 46 +69	49 65 +77	27 34 +46
4.	23 23 31 +22	28 17 23 +44	91 22 34 +51	72 54 36 +21	78 52 43 +45	33 25 36 +21
5.	423 101 +324	526 345 +116	123 541 +162	752 348 +150	429 316 541 +302	324 115 462 +115

Subtract.

	a	*b*	*c*	*d*	*e*
6.	752 −341	673 −424	583 −193	765 −489	605 −329
7.	4723 −221	5806 −447	3924 −163	7811 −912	6425 −587

Perfect score: 40   My score: _____

Lesson 1   Addition

Add the ones.

Add the tens.

67	7			67	67
98	8 ⟩ 15			98	98
+83	+3 +3			+83	+83
	18 or 10 + 8		8		248

Add.

	a	*b*	*c*	*d*	*e*	*f*
1.	4 5 +7	6 8 +9	5 2 +8	9 8 +3	4 6 +5	7 7 +6
2.	1 0 4 0 3 0 +5 0	2 0 6 0 5 0 +6 0	1 0 2 0 9 0 +4 0	2 0 4 0 3 0 +7 0	1 0 5 0 6 0 +4 0	2 0 7 0 5 0 +8 0
3.	4 4 3 5 +5 7	6 6 5 8 +5 9	2 5 9 2 +4 8	4 9 3 8 +7 3	5 4 6 6 +4 5	7 7 5 7 +8 6
4.	2 5 3 2 +4 1	2 7 3 5 +4 2	5 5 5 5 +5 5	3 2 4 4 +2 8	7 5 1 6 +5 8	2 2 1 4 +9 1
5.	5 7 2 8 +3 6	4 2 5 4 +7 8	7 9 3 4 +2 9	6 8 7 8 +8 8	2 5 3 6 +4 2	5 3 2 6 +1 3
6.	4 5 1 8 +5 2	6 1 2 9 +5 8	8 3 7 6 +1 9	4 9 4 2 +4 3	3 7 6 7 +2 6	9 8 1 6 +3 5

Perfect score: 36   My score: _____

59

Problem Solving

NATIONAL LEAGUE TEAM STANDINGS		
TEAM	WON	LOST
CUBS	72	43
CARDS	69	48
METS	64	52
PIRATES	58	55
PHILLIES	44	68
EXPOS	37	79

Solve each problem.

1. How many games have been won by the first three teams in the National League?

The Cubs have won _____ games.

The Cards have won _____ games.

The Mets have won _____ games.

Together they have won _____ games.

2. How many games have been lost by the last three teams in the National League?

The Pirates have lost _____ games.

The Phillies have lost _____ games.

The Expos have lost _____ games.

Together they have lost _____ games.

3. How many games have been won by the Cubs, Mets, Phillies, and Expos?

The Cubs, Mets, Phillies,
   and Expos have won _____ games.

4. How many games have the Cubs, Cards, and Pirates lost?

The Cubs, Cards, and
   Pirates have lost _____ games.

1.

2.

3.

4.

Perfect score: 10   My score: _____

60

Lesson 2   Addition

	Add the ones.	Add the tens.	Add the hundreds.
642	6¹42	^{2 1}642	^{2 1}642
156	156	156	156
275	275	275	275
+143	+143	+143	+143
	6	16	1216

$2 + 6 + 5 + 3 =$ ____ | $10 + 40 + 50 + 70 + 40 =$ _____ | $200 + 600 + 100 + 200 + 100 =$ _____

$16 = 10 +$ ____ | $210 = 200 +$ _____ | $1200 = 1000 +$ _____

Add.

	a	b	c	d	e	f
1.	372 456 +174	382 154 +283	231 336 +136	152 443 +178	321 305 +238	143 116 +212
2.	425 641 +703	443 217 +602	613 247 +138	574 142 +281	382 425 +678	392 456 +731
3.	728 365 +428	639 752 +417	618 304 +120	856 174 +372	564 345 +654	224 305 +406
4.	421 145 162 +231	178 214 103 +407	513 223 641 +412	421 146 273 +154	762 531 444 +258	372 541 635 +413
5.	603 254 316 +222	425 245 542 +254	631 211 431 +222	731 240 635 +214	245 361 524 +113	284 563 711 +245

Perfect score: 30   My score: _____

Problem Solving

Solve each problem.

1. The local theater had a special Saturday movie. They sold 175 tickets to men, 142 to women, and 327 to children. How many tickets did they sell in all?

They sold _____ tickets to men.

They sold _____ tickets to women.

They sold _____ tickets to children.

They sold _____ tickets in all.

2. In the local high school there are 768 boys, 829 girls, and 107 teachers. How many teachers and pupils are there in all?

There are _____ boys.

There are _____ girls.

There are _____ teachers.

There are _____ teachers and pupils in all.

3. The number of people living in 4 different apartment buildings is 203, 245, 268, and 275. How many people live in all 4 buildings?

_____ people live in all 4 buildings.

4. A living room floor has 195 tiles. A bedroom floor has 168 tiles. A kitchen floor has 144 tiles. How many tiles are in the 3 rooms?

There are _____ tiles in these 3 rooms.

1.	
2.	
3.	4.

Perfect score: 10   My score: _____

62

Lesson 3   Subtraction

Rename 40 as "3 tens and 10 ones." Then subtract the ones.

Rename 7 hundreds and 3 tens as "6 hundreds and 13 tens." Then subtract the tens.

Subtract the hundreds.

```
    740        740        740        740
   −271       −271       −271       −271
                  9         69        469
```

Subtract.

	a	b	c	d	e	f
1.	5 3 4 −2 7 3	2 6 3 −1 5 4	7 5 8 −4 3 9	4 5 0 −2 6 1	5 3 6 −3 4 7	2 7 4 −1 5 4
2.	4 6 3 −3 7 2	7 8 2 −2 3 4	5 9 4 −2 8 7	6 8 1 −3 8 2	3 8 4 −1 7 5	8 0 6 −7 6 4
3.	7 6 4 −1 3 7	6 3 5 −4 4 7	4 9 2 −1 1 3	7 8 0 −1 5 2	4 4 4 −2 3 5	5 6 2 −3 5 7
4.	8 3 6 −2 5 7	9 4 4 −2 5 6	7 5 8 −1 6 7	5 0 4 −2 3 5	6 7 2 −2 8 5	8 9 2 −2 8 4
5.	9 4 5 −4 6 3	3 7 8 −1 2 6	5 6 4 −2 4 3	8 3 9 −2 5 7	2 4 5 −1 4 6	7 7 6 −3 8 2
6.	8 0 5 −3 0 8	9 0 0 −7 5 0	7 6 4 −3 4 5	8 4 0 −4 2 6	9 5 5 −7 6 5	4 3 6 −3 2 7

Perfect score: 36   My score: _____

Problem Solving

Solve each problem.

1. Babe Ruth hit 714 home runs. Ted Williams hit 521 home runs. How many more home runs did Babe Ruth hit than Ted Williams?

Babe Ruth hit _____ home runs.

Ted Williams hit _____ home runs.

Babe Ruth hit _____ more home runs than Ted Williams.

2. A train has 850 seats. There are 317 empty seats. How many people are seated?

The train has _____ seats.

_____ seats are empty.

There are _____ people seated.

3. Hoover Dam is 726 feet high. Folsom Dam is 340 feet high. How much higher is Hoover Dam than Folsom Dam?

Hoover Dam is _____ feet high.

Folsom Dam is _____ feet high.

Hoover Dam is _____ feet higher than Folsom Dam.

4. The quarterback threw 247 passes. Only 138 passes were caught. How many were not caught?

_____ passes were not caught.

5. A meeting room can hold 443 people. There are 268 people in the room now. How many more people can it hold?

It can hold _____ more people.

1.

2.

3.

4.

5.

Perfect score: 11   My score: _____

Lesson 4   Subtraction

	Subtract the ones.	Rename 2 hundreds and 5 tens as "1 hundred and 15 tens." Subtract the tens.	Rename 4 thousands and 1 hundred as "3 thousands and 11 hundreds." Subtract the hundreds.	Subtract the thousands.
4253 −281	425̸3 −281 2	¹ ¹⁵ 42̸5̸3 −281 72	³¹ ¹ ¹⁵ 4̸2̸5̸3 281 972	³¹ ¹ ¹⁵ 4̸2̸5̸3 −281 3972

Subtract.

	a	b	c	d	e
1.	7 5 4 3 − 2 1 1	6 8 1 3 − 4 0 2	7 2 5 4 − 1 3 2	4 9 3 6 − 7 2 6	2 8 1 5 − 8 1 3
2.	3 5 6 2 − 2 3 5	4 2 5 3 − 1 4 7	6 5 4 1 − 5 3 8	3 4 7 3 − 2 5 5	5 4 9 6 − 3 3 9
3.	3 7 1 0 − 3 4 0	9 6 4 2 − 2 7 1	3 8 1 7 − 4 5 4	5 2 1 6 − 1 8 2	3 8 4 7 − 3 7 7
4.	4 2 9 5 − 7 2 4	4 0 0 7 − 8 0 5	8 2 8 1 − 4 7 0	5 5 5 4 − 6 4 4	6 3 8 2 − 8 8 2
5.	5 9 8 6 − 5 3 7	2 4 1 3 − 8 2 9	4 5 0 7 − 7 5 8	3 1 5 4 − 2 0 5	2 6 4 0 − 8 3 4
6.	8 3 2 9 − 4 7 5	7 6 0 4 − 8 2 9	3 9 8 7 − 9 8 8	4 2 0 5 − 7 3 6	1 3 8 3 − 5 2 9

Perfect score: 30   My score: _____

Problem Solving

Solve each problem.

1. Ms. Ramos bought a car that cost 3,165 dollars. She paid 875 dollars. How much does she still owe?

The new car cost _____ dollars.

Ms. Ramos paid _____ dollars.

She still owes _____ dollars.

2. Mount Whitney is 4,418 meters high. Mount Davis is 979 meters high. How much higher is Mount Whitney?

Mount Whitney is _____ meters high.

Mount Davis is _____ meters high.

Mount Whitney is _____ meters higher.

3. There are 1,156 pupils enrolled in a school. Today 219 pupils are absent. How many are present?

_____ pupils are present.

4. There are 5,280 feet in a mile. John walked 895 feet. How many more feet must he go to walk a mile?

He must go _____ more feet to walk a mile.

5. Henry's family went 2,198 kilometers in 5 days. They went 843 kilometers the first 2 days. How many kilometers did they go in the last 3 days?

They went _____ kilometers in the last three days.

6. There are 1,255 people on a police force. If 596 are women, how many are men?

There are _____ men.

1.

2.

3.

4.

5.

6.

Perfect score: 10   My score: _____

CHAPTER 5 TEST

Add.

	a	*b*	*c*	*d*	*e*
1.	3 2 +5	4 7 +6	8 4 +9	7 0 3 0 5 0 +4 0	5 0 7 0 8 0 +3 0
2.	3 5 2 4 +2 0	5 7 1 3 +2 8	7 4 8 2 +3 6	2 3 3 2 5 8 +4 2	4 2 5 3 6 4 +7 0
3.	4 2 1 3 1 2 +1 4 8	6 2 3 1 7 4 +1 6 2	4 7 3 1 2 6 +2 4 8	3 2 6 1 1 2 2 2 4 +6 0 7	5 2 6 3 8 1 4 2 6 +5 4 3

Subtract.

	a	*b*	*c*	*d*
4.	7 6 5 − 2 4 3	2 9 0 − 1 8 3	8 4 6 − 3 5 4	8 4 6 − 2 9 7
5.	5 8 3 6 − 3 1 4	7 5 4 2 − 2 7 5	6 0 3 9 − 2 6 8	2 5 6 0 − 7 6 4

Solve each problem.

6. Four girls earned the following points in a contest: 145, 387, 245, and 197. What was the total number of points earned?

The total number of points was _____.

7. Ralph's new car was driven 837 miles. Jo's new car was driven 3275 miles. How many more miles was Jo's new car driven than Ralph's?

Jo's car was driven _____ more miles.

6.

7.

Perfect score: 25   My score: _____

67

PRE-TEST—Measurement

Complete the following.

a	b

1. There are _____ days in a year.   4:10 means 10 minutes after _____.

2. There are _____ days in a leap year. 3:50 means 10 minutes to _____.

3. There are _____ days in April.   5:45 means _____ minutes after 5.

4. There are _____ days in March.   5:45 means _____ minutes to 6.

Complete the following as shown.

a	b	c

5.   XI = __11__   V = _____   IV = _____

6. XVII = _____   XXVI = _____   XIX = _____

7.   7 = __VII__   10 = _____   9 = _____

8.   24 = _____   31 = _____   25 = _____

Add or subtract.

	a	b	c	d	e
9.	$5.2 0 +6.8 9	$1 2.6 5 +1.2 5	4 6¢ +3 7¢	2 9¢ 3 7¢ +2 8¢	$ 3.7 3 .2 8 +1 4.5 0
10.	$1 6.5 0 −3.2 5	$1 4.7 5 −2.9 0	$7.4 0 −.8 4	5 6¢ −3 8¢	9 7¢ −5 0¢

Solve.

11. Ms. Romanez bought a saw for $21.95 and a hammer for $9.49. She paid $1.88 tax. How much was her total bill?

Her total bill was _____.

Perfect score: 29   My score: _____

Lesson 1 Reading Our Calendar

NAME _____

JANUARY

S	M	T	W	T	F	S
						1
2	3	4	5	6	7	8
9	10	11	12	13	14	15
16	17	18	19	20	21	22
23	24	25	26	27	28	29
30	31					

FEBRUARY

S	M	T	W	T	F	S
		1	2	3	4	5
6	7	8	9	10	11	12
13	14	15	16	17	18	19
20	21	22	23	24	25	26
27	28					

MARCH

S	M	T	W	T	F	S
		1	2	3	4	5
6	7	8	9	10	11	12
13	14	15	16	17	18	19
20	21	22	23	24	25	26
27	28	29	30	31		

APRIL

S	M	T	W	T	F	S
					1	2
3	4	5	6	7	8	9
10	11	12	13	14	15	16
17	18	19	20	21	22	23
24	25	26	27	28	29	30

MAY

S	M	T	W	T	F	S
1	2	3	4	5	6	7
8	9	10	11	12	13	14
15	16	17	18	19	20	21
22	23	24	25	26	27	28
29	30	31				

JUNE

S	M	T	W	T	F	S
			1	2	3	4
5	6	7	8	9	10	11
12	13	14	15	16	17	18
19	20	21	22	23	24	25
26	27	28	29	30		

JULY

S	M	T	W	T	F	S
					1	2
3	4	5	6	7	8	9
10	11	12	13	14	15	16
17	18	19	20	21	22	23
24	25	26	27	28	29	30
31						

AUGUST

S	M	T	W	T	F	S
	1	2	3	4	5	6
7	8	9	10	11	12	13
14	15	16	17	18	19	20
21	22	23	24	25	26	27
28	29	30	31			

SEPTEMBER

S	M	T	W	T	F	S
				1	2	3
4	5	6	7	8	9	10
11	12	13	14	15	16	17
18	19	20	21	22	23	24
25	26	27	28	29	30	

OCTOBER

S	M	T	W	T	F	S
						1
2	3	4	5	6	7	8
9	10	11	12	13	14	15
16	17	18	19	20	21	22
23	24	25	26	27	28	29
30	31					

NOVEMBER

S	M	T	W	T	F	S
		1	2	3	4	5
6	7	8	9	10	11	12
13	14	15	16	17	18	19
20	21	22	23	24	25	26
27	28	29	30			

DECEMBER

S	M	T	W	T	F	S
				1	2	3
4	5	6	7	8	9	10
11	12	13	14	15	16	17
18	19	20	21	22	23	24
25	26	27	28	29	30	31

There are 365 days in the calendar year shown. Every four years, there are 366 days in a year. It is called a **leap year**. Only in a leap year is there a February 29.

There are ___31___ days in March.   There are _____ days in June.

March 1 is on ___Tuesday___ .   June 1 is on _____.

On the calendar above, April has _4_ Sundays and ____ Saturdays.

Answer each question. Use the calendar to help you.

a   *b*

1. How many days are in July? _____   On what day is July 1? _____

2. How many Tuesdays are in November? _____   How many Wednesdays are in November? _____

3. How many months have 30 days? _____   How many months have 31 days? _____

4. What date is the 3rd Thursday in August? _____   What date is the 2nd Monday in April? _____

5. How many days of the year have passed when we reach May 1? _____   What date falls forty-five days before December 25? _____

Perfect score: 10   My score: _____

69

Lesson 2   Telling Time

{ 7:10 is read "seven ten" and means "10 minutes after 7."

7:10

{ 3:40 is read "three forty" and means "40 minutes after 3" or "20 minutes to 4."

3:40

{ 8:55 is read "eight fifty-five" and means "55 minutes after _____"

or "_____ minutes to _____."

8:55

Complete the following.

	a	*b*
1.	3:05 means _____ minutes after _____.	6:50 means _____ minutes to _____.
2.	10:20 means _____ minutes after _____.	11:35 means _____ minutes to _____.
3.	8:45 means _____ minutes after _____.	8:45 means _____ minutes to _____.
4.	5:30 means _____ minutes after _____.	5:30 means _____ minutes to _____.
5.	1:10 means _____ minutes after _____.	12:55 means _____ minutes to _____.

For each clockface, write the numerals that name the time.

	a	*b*	*c*	*d*

6.

_____ : _____   _____ : _____   _____ : _____   _____ : _____

7.

_____ : _____   _____ : _____   _____ : _____   _____ : _____

Perfect score: 28   My score: _____

Lesson 3   Roman Numerals

I means 1. V means 5. X means 10.

II means $1+1$ or 2. III means $1+1+1$ or 3.

VI means $5+1$ or 6. IV means $5-1$ or 4.

XXV means $10+10+5$ or 25. IX means $10-1$ or 9.

VII means $5+1+$ _____ or _____. XXI means $10+$ _____ $+1$ or _____.

XIV means _____ $+4$ or _____. XIX means _____ $+9$ or _____.

Complete the following as shown.

	a	b	c	d
1.	XXIV = 24	XX = ____	XII = ____	VIII = ____
2.	IV = ____	XXVI = ____	XVII = ____	XXXI = ____
3.	XXXVI = ____	XXIX = ____	XI = ____	XXXIII = ____
4.	XVIII = ____	IX = ____	XXXIV = ____	XIII = ____
5.	V = ____	XXV = ____	VI = ____	XXI = ____
6.	XXXVIII = ____	XXXV = ____	XXVII = ____	XVI = ____
7.	XXIII = ____	XXXVII = ____	XIV = ____	XXXII = ____

Write a Roman numeral for each of the following.

	a	b	c
8.	3 = _____	7 = _____	15 = _____
9.	19 = _____	22 = _____	28 = _____
10.	30 = _____	20 = _____	39 = _____

Perfect score: 36   My score: _____

Lesson 4   Money

1 penny	1 nickel	1 dime	1 quarter	1 dollar
1 cent	5 cents	10 cents	25 cents	100 cents
1¢ or $.01	5¢ or $.05	10¢ or $.10	25¢ or $.25	$1.00

25 pennies have a value of ____25____ cents or ____1____ quarter.

5 pennies have a value of _____ cents or _____ nickel.

$2.57 means ____2____ dollars and ____57____ cents.

$3.45 means _____ dollars and _____ cents.

Complete the following.

1.   10 pennies have a value of _____ cents or _____ nickels.

2.   10 pennies have a value of _____ cents or _____ dime.

3.   20 pennies have a value of _____ cents or _____ dimes.

4.   15 pennies have a value of _____ cents or _____ nickels.

5.   20 pennies have a value of _____ cents or _____ nickels.

Complete the following as shown.

6. $14.05 means _____ dollars and _____ cents.

7. $12.70 means _____ dollars and _____ cents.

8. $8.14 means _____ dollars and _____ cents.

9. $.65 means _____ dollars and _____ cents.

10. $10.01 means _____ dollars and _____ cents.

Perfect score: 18   My score: _____

Lesson 5   Money

	$12.00				
$9.05	.45	45¢	$ .75	$14.08	$13.00
+6.98	+3.16	+38¢	+.38	−7.25	−6.05
$16.03	$15.61	83¢	$1.13	$6.83	$6.95

Add or subtract as usual.

Put a decimal point (.) and a $ or ¢ in the answer.

Be sure to line up the decimal points.

Add or subtract.

	a	b	c	d	e
1.	$ .3 6 +1 2.4 0	$3.7 5 +1.4 6	$ 1.3 6 +4 0.0 0	3 7¢ +5 8¢	$4.3 5 +.2 7
2.	$5.2 0 −3.1 8	$1 2.6 4 −5.0 8	$3.0 0 −.5 4	8 8¢ −7 6¢	$2 4.4 2 −1.6 8
3.	$ 4.2 3 1 6.9 0 +.8 9	$7.2 5 .4 0 +4.4 2	$ 8.0 5 1 2.1 6 +.5 8	4 7¢ 1 8¢ +2 5¢	$ .0 8 3.6 7 +1 4.3 0
4.	$1 5.4 0 −3.6 2	$5.7 0 −2.0 8	$1 1.3 0 −.8 6	9 1¢ −7 5¢	$1 7.2 0 −4.0 6
5.	$2 7.0 0 −1 3.4 5	$6 5.2 1 +3.8 0	$ .1 2 +1.8 8	4 7¢ −1 9¢	$3.0 0 −1.7 8
6.	$1 6.4 9 +2 8.9 8	$4 0.6 0 −7.5 6	$5.0 0 −2.7 2	3 8¢ +3 5¢	$8.7 5 +.6 4

Perfect score: 30   My score: _____

Problem Solving

Solve each problem.

1. Eileen's mother bought a dress for $22.98 and a blouse for $17.64. How much did these items cost altogether?

They cost _____ altogether.

2. Find the total cost of a basketball at $18.69, a baseball at $8.05, and a football at $24.98.

The total cost is _____.

3. Joe has $2.50. Mike has $1.75. Joe has how much more money than Mike?

Joe has _____ more than Mike.

4. In problem 2, how much more does the basketball cost than the baseball? How much more does the football cost than the basketball?

The basketball costs _____ more than
   the baseball.

The football costs _____ more than
   the basketball.

5. Charlotte saved $4.20 one week, $.90 the next week, and $2.05 the third week. How much money did she save during these 3 weeks?

Charlotte saved _____ in 3 weeks.

6. Mr. Lewis paid $4.45 for fruit. He paid $.99 for potatoes. The tax was $.33. How much was the total bill?

His total bill was _____.

7. Gary wants to buy a 95¢ whistle. He now has 68¢. How much more money does he need to buy the whistle?

Gary needs _____ more.

1.	2.
3.	
4.	
5.	**6.**
7.	

Perfect score: 8   My score: _____

74

CHAPTER 6 TEST

Answer each question. Use the calendar to help you.

	May					
S	M	T	W	T	F	S
		1	2	3	4	5
6	7	8	9	10	11	12
13	14	15	16	17	18	19
20	21	22	23	24	25	26
27	28	29	30	31		

1. How many days are in May? _____

2. On what day is May 4? _____

For each clockface, write the numerals that name the time.

        a   *b*   *c*

3.

_____:_____   _____:_____   _____:_____

Complete the following as shown.

    a   *b*   *c*

4. XVI = _____16_____   IX = _____   XXXII = _____

5. 14 = _____XIV_____   8 = _____   29 = _____

Add or subtract.

	a	*b*	*c*	*d*	*e*
6.	$1 5.3 2 +1 6.4 5	$3.2 4 +.7 3	4 2¢ +5 4¢	1 6¢ 3 7¢ +2 0¢	$ .6 2 1 3.4 0 +1.6 8
7.	$3.5 2 −2.1 7	$1 3.1 4 −5.3 3	9 3¢ −3 9¢	$1 7.5 0 −1.0 9	$5.1 4 −1.0 8

Solve.

8. Maria needs $54.68 to buy a coat she wants. She now has $50.75. How much more money does she need to buy the coat?

Maria needs _____ more.

Perfect score: 20   My score: _____

PRE-TEST—Multiplication

Multiply.

	a	b	c	d	e	f
1.	5 ×2	7 ×2	2 ×2	6 ×2	4 ×2	9 ×2
2.	3 ×3	5 ×3	4 ×3	7 ×3	9 ×3	2 ×3
3.	7 ×0	5 ×0	0 ×4	0 ×6	3 ×0	0 ×8
4.	3 ×1	7 ×1	1 ×4	1 ×1	5 ×1	1 ×8
5.	7 ×4	3 ×4	9 ×4	6 ×4	5 ×4	4 ×4
6.	8 ×5	6 ×5	9 ×5	4 ×5	3 ×5	2 ×5
7.	9 ×0	8 ×4	6 ×3	0 ×1	5 ×5	0 ×3
8.	1 ×9	2 ×4	1 ×2	7 ×5	8 ×3	2 ×1
9.	3 ×2	1 ×3	0 ×7	8 ×2	1 ×6	1 ×5

Perfect score: 54   My score: _____

Lesson 1   Multiplication

2×3 is read "two times three." 2×3 means $3+3$.
3×2 is read "three times two." 3×2 means $2+2+2$.
4×5 is read "four times five." 4×5 means $5+5+5+5$.

3×6 is read "three times six." 3×6 means $6 + 6 + 6$.

2×7 is read "two times seven." 2×7 means $7 + 7$.

Complete the following as shown.

1. 2×5 is read _____

2. 3×4 is read _____

3. 5×2 is read _____

4. 4×8 is read _____

5. 4×7 is read _____

Complete the following as shown.

	a	*b*
6.	2×4 means _____	4×2 means _____
7.	3×5 means _____	5×3 means _____
8.	3×7 means _____	7×3 means _____
9.	4×6 means _____	6×4 means _____
10.	2×8 means _____	8×2 means _____
11.	3×9 means _____	9×3 means _____

Perfect score: 17   My score: _____

77

Lesson 2   Multiplication

3×4 means $4 + 4 + 4$. 4×3 means $3 + 3 + 3 + 3$.

$$
\begin{array}{r} 4 \\ \times 3 \\ \hline 12 \end{array}
\qquad
\begin{array}{r} 4 \\ 4 \\ +4 \\ \hline 12 \end{array}
\qquad
\begin{array}{r} 3 \\ \times 4 \\ \hline 12 \end{array}
\qquad
\begin{array}{r} 3 \\ 3 \\ 3 \\ +3 \\ \hline 12 \end{array}
$$

Add or multiply.

	a	b	c	d	e	f
1.	8 +8	8 ×2	4 +4	4 ×2	5 +5	5 ×2
2.	6 +6	6 ×2	7 +7	7 ×2	2 +2	2 ×2
3.	9 +9	9 ×2	3 +3	3 ×2	1 +1	1 ×2
4.	2 2 +2	2 ×3	3 3 +3	3 ×3	4 4 +4	4 ×3
5.	5 5 +5	5 ×3	6 6 +6	6 ×3	7 7 +7	7 ×3
6.	8 8 +8	8 ×3	9 9 +9	9 ×3	1 1 +1	1 ×3

Perfect score: 36   My score: _____

Lesson 3   Multiplication

1 ×0	2 ×0	0 ×3	0 ×4	0 ×1	1 ×1	2 ×1	1 ×3
0	0	0	0	0	1	2	3

Multiply.

	a	b	c	d	e	f
1.	0 ×2	9 ×1	1 ×7	6 ×0	1 ×5	0 ×7
2.	4 ×0	8 ×1	1 ×4	0 ×9	7 ×0	6 ×1
3.	5 ×0	0 ×8	5 ×1	1 ×6	1 ×1	8 ×0
4.	1 ×7	0 ×4	3 ×0	9 ×0	7 ×1	1 ×5
5.	0 ×7	1 ×9	1 ×6	0 ×5	1 ×0	2 ×1
6.	1 ×4	1 ×8	4 ×0	8 ×1	0 ×6	0 ×3
7.	0 ×9	6 ×1	0 ×2	9 ×1	0 ×1	3 ×1
8.	1 ×2	6 ×0	7 ×0	1 ×3	4 ×1	0 ×0

Perfect score: 48   My score: _____

Problem Solving

Solve each problem.

1. Molly bought 2 baseball cards. Each baseball card cost 9 cents. How much did Molly pay for the baseball cards?

Molly bought _____ baseball cards.

Each baseball card cost _____ cents.

Molly paid _____ cents for the baseball cards.

2. Bob bought 2 football cards. They cost 6 cents each. How much did Bob pay for the football cards?

Bob bought _____ football cards.

One football card cost _____ cents.

Bob paid _____ cents for the football cards.

3. There are 8 cards in each pack. How many cards are in 3 packs?

_____ cards are in three packs.

4. One basketball card costs 5 cents. How much will 8 basketball cards cost?

Eight basketball cards will cost _____ cents.

1.

2.

3.

4.

Perfect score: 8   My score: _____

Lesson 4   Multiplication

4-column →

x	0	1	2	3	4	5	6	7	8	9
0	0	0	0	0	0	0	0	0	0	0
1	0	1	2	3	4	5	6	7	8	9
2	0	2	4	6	8	10	12	14	16	18
3	0	3	6	9	12	15	18	21	24	27
4	0	4	8	12	16	20	24	28	32	36
5	0	5	10	15	20	25	30	35	40	45
6	0	6	12	18	24	30				
7	0	7	14	21	28	35				
8	0	8	16	24	32	40				
9	0	9	18	27	36	45				

6-row →

```
  6  ──→ Find the 6 -row.
× 4  ──→ Find the 4 -column.
 ───
 24  ←── The product is named where
         the 6-row and 4-column meet.
```

Multiply.

	a	b	c	d	e	f
1.	5 ×4	8 ×4	7 ×5	6 ×5	2 ×4	4 ×3
2.	5 ×5	6 ×3	9 ×4	1 ×4	0 ×5	4 ×4
3.	3 ×5	7 ×4	2 ×5	4 ×2	8 ×5	9 ×2
4.	5 ×3	3 ×3	8 ×2	0 ×4	3 ×2	5 ×2
5.	6 ×4	8 ×3	4 ×1	5 ×0	5 ×1	6 ×2
6.	9 ×5	4 ×0	3 ×4	7 ×2	7 ×3	1 ×5

Perfect score: 36   My score: _____

Problem Solving

Solve each problem.

1. Yvonne wants to buy 5 erasers. They cost 9 cents each. How much will she have to pay?

Yvonne wants to buy _____ erasers.

One eraser costs _____ cents.

Yvonne will have to pay _____ cents.

2. There are 5 rows of mailboxes. There are 7 mailboxes in each row. How many mailboxes are there in all?

There are _____ mailboxes in each row.

There are _____ rows of mailboxes.

There are _____ mailboxes in all.

3. Milton, the pet monkey, eats 4 meals every day. How many meals does he eat in a week?

There are _____ days in a week.

Milton eats _____ meals every day.

Milton eats _____ meals in a week.

4. In a baseball game each team gets 3 outs per inning. How many outs does each team get in a 5-inning game?

There are _____ innings in the game.

Each team gets _____ outs per inning.

The team gets _____ outs in the 5-inning game.

5. Howard has gained 4 pounds in each of the past 5 months. How much weight has he gained?

Howard has gained _____ pounds in 4 months.

1.	
2.	
3.	
4.	5.

Perfect score: 13   My score: _____

82

Lesson 5   Multiplication

Multiply.

	a	b	c	d	e	f
1.	$\begin{array}{r} 0 \\ \times 8 \\ \hline \end{array}$	$\begin{array}{r} 4 \\ \times 2 \\ \hline \end{array}$	$\begin{array}{r} 8 \\ \times 5 \\ \hline \end{array}$	$\begin{array}{r} 7 \\ \times 3 \\ \hline \end{array}$	$\begin{array}{r} 6 \\ \times 1 \\ \hline \end{array}$	$\begin{array}{r} 7 \\ \times 0 \\ \hline \end{array}$
2.	$\begin{array}{r} 1 \\ \times 1 \\ \hline \end{array}$	$\begin{array}{r} 9 \\ \times 2 \\ \hline \end{array}$	$\begin{array}{r} 4 \\ \times 4 \\ \hline \end{array}$	$\begin{array}{r} 3 \\ \times 5 \\ \hline \end{array}$	$\begin{array}{r} 6 \\ \times 5 \\ \hline \end{array}$	$\begin{array}{r} 1 \\ \times 4 \\ \hline \end{array}$
3.	$\begin{array}{r} 0 \\ \times 6 \\ \hline \end{array}$	$\begin{array}{r} 1 \\ \times 2 \\ \hline \end{array}$	$\begin{array}{r} 4 \\ \times 0 \\ \hline \end{array}$	$\begin{array}{r} 8 \\ \times 2 \\ \hline \end{array}$	$\begin{array}{r} 9 \\ \times 5 \\ \hline \end{array}$	$\begin{array}{r} 5 \\ \times 5 \\ \hline \end{array}$
4.	$\begin{array}{r} 8 \\ \times 4 \\ \hline \end{array}$	$\begin{array}{r} 6 \\ \times 3 \\ \hline \end{array}$	$\begin{array}{r} 1 \\ \times 5 \\ \hline \end{array}$	$\begin{array}{r} 9 \\ \times 0 \\ \hline \end{array}$	$\begin{array}{r} 2 \\ \times 1 \\ \hline \end{array}$	$\begin{array}{r} 7 \\ \times 2 \\ \hline \end{array}$
5.	$\begin{array}{r} 5 \\ \times 3 \\ \hline \end{array}$	$\begin{array}{r} 7 \\ \times 4 \\ \hline \end{array}$	$\begin{array}{r} 4 \\ \times 5 \\ \hline \end{array}$	$\begin{array}{r} 3 \\ \times 2 \\ \hline \end{array}$	$\begin{array}{r} 9 \\ \times 3 \\ \hline \end{array}$	$\begin{array}{r} 8 \\ \times 1 \\ \hline \end{array}$
6.	$\begin{array}{r} 6 \\ \times 0 \\ \hline \end{array}$	$\begin{array}{r} 3 \\ \times 1 \\ \hline \end{array}$	$\begin{array}{r} 6 \\ \times 2 \\ \hline \end{array}$	$\begin{array}{r} 0 \\ \times 0 \\ \hline \end{array}$	$\begin{array}{r} 2 \\ \times 3 \\ \hline \end{array}$	$\begin{array}{r} 9 \\ \times 4 \\ \hline \end{array}$
7.	$\begin{array}{r} 7 \\ \times 5 \\ \hline \end{array}$	$\begin{array}{r} 8 \\ \times 3 \\ \hline \end{array}$	$\begin{array}{r} 1 \\ \times 0 \\ \hline \end{array}$	$\begin{array}{r} 0 \\ \times 3 \\ \hline \end{array}$	$\begin{array}{r} 4 \\ \times 1 \\ \hline \end{array}$	$\begin{array}{r} 6 \\ \times 4 \\ \hline \end{array}$
8.	$\begin{array}{r} 5 \\ \times 4 \\ \hline \end{array}$	$\begin{array}{r} 2 \\ \times 2 \\ \hline \end{array}$	$\begin{array}{r} 9 \\ \times 1 \\ \hline \end{array}$	$\begin{array}{r} 1 \\ \times 7 \\ \hline \end{array}$	$\begin{array}{r} 2 \\ \times 4 \\ \hline \end{array}$	$\begin{array}{r} 3 \\ \times 3 \\ \hline \end{array}$
9.	$\begin{array}{r} 1 \\ \times 9 \\ \hline \end{array}$	$\begin{array}{r} 2 \\ \times 0 \\ \hline \end{array}$	$\begin{array}{r} 5 \\ \times 2 \\ \hline \end{array}$	$\begin{array}{r} 3 \\ \times 4 \\ \hline \end{array}$	$\begin{array}{r} 2 \\ \times 5 \\ \hline \end{array}$	$\begin{array}{r} 4 \\ \times 3 \\ \hline \end{array}$

Perfect score: 54   My score: _____

Problem Solving

Solve each problem.

1. Neal has 6 books. Each book weighs 1 kilogram. What is the weight of all the books?

Neal has _____ books.

Each book weighs _____ kilogram.

The six books weigh _____ kilograms.

2. A baseball game has 4 time periods. Amy's team is to play 8 games. How many periods will her team play?

Amy's team is to play _____ games.

Each game has _____ time periods.

Amy's team will play _____ time periods in all.

3. Ellen works 8 hours every day. How many hours does she work in 5 days?

She works _____ hours in 5 days.

4. Chuck can ride his bicycle 5 miles in an hour. At that speed how far could he ride in 2 hours?

Chuck could ride _____ miles in 2 hours.

5. Calvin bought 5 bags of balloons. Each bag had 6 balloons. How many balloons did he buy?

Calvin bought _____ balloons in all.

6. Eve can build a model car in 3 hours. How long would it take her to build 4 model cars?

Eve could build 4 model cars in _____ hours.

1.

2.

3.

4.

5.

6.

Perfect score: 10   My score: _____

CHAPTER 7 TEST

Multiply.

	a	*b*	*c*	*d*	*e*
1.	1 ×6	7 ×4	9 ×0	3 ×4	9 ×5
2.	4 ×3	7 ×3	0 ×6	1 ×4	6 ×2
3.	9 ×2	8 ×5	9 ×3	3 ×2	4 ×4
4.	0 ×1	5 ×5	9 ×4	3 ×0	4 ×5

Solve each problem.

5. John bought 5 boxes of pencils. There are 6 pencils in each box. How many pencils did he buy?

John bought _____ boxes of pencils.

There are _____ pencils in each box.

He bought _____ pencils in all.

6. Linda is to put 4 apples in each bag. How many apples does she need to fill 8 bags?

Linda needs _____ apples in all.

7. Troy bought 3 boxes of crayons. Each box held 8 crayons. How many crayons did he buy?

Troy bought _____ crayons.

5.

6.

7.

Perfect score: 25   My score: _____

PRE-TEST—Multiplication

Multiply.

	a	b	c	d	e	f
1.	7 ×6	6 ×6	4 ×6	8 ×6	5 ×6	9 ×6
2.	8 ×7	4 ×7	9 ×7	7 ×7	6 ×7	5 ×7
3.	9 ×8	5 ×8	7 ×8	8 ×8	6 ×8	4 ×8
4.	6 ×9	9 ×9	5 ×9	8 ×9	4 ×9	7 ×9

Solve each problem.

5. Andrew set up 9 rows of chairs. He put 9 chairs in each row. How many chairs did he use?

Andrew used _____ chairs.

6. Sarah's dad works 7 hours every day. How many hours would he work in 8 days?

He would work _____ hours in 8 days.

7. There are 9 players on a team. How many players are there on 7 teams?

There are _____ players in all.

8. Paul puts 6 apples into each bag. How many apples does he need to fill 7 bags?

He would need _____ apples.

5.

6.

7.

8.

Perfect score: 28   My score: _____

Lesson 1   Multiplication

NAME _____

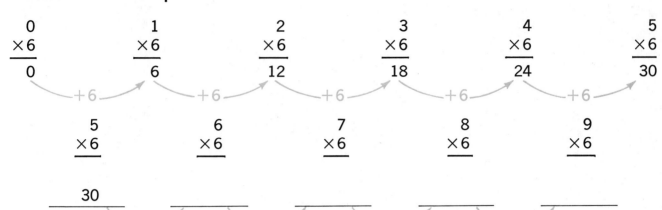

Multiply.

	a	b	c	d	e	f
1.	5 ×6	3 ×3	9 ×6	8 ×4	0 ×5	5 ×3
2.	8 ×5	2 ×6	6 ×4	5 ×5	3 ×4	6 ×1
3.	4 ×3	7 ×4	6 ×5	8 ×6	9 ×4	8 ×3
4.	0 ×3	3 ×6	1 ×5	4 ×4	2 ×3	4 ×5
5.	7 ×6	9 ×5	7 ×5	0 ×4	5 ×2	2 ×4
6.	6 ×6	6 ×2	5 ×4	1 ×3	3 ×5	0 ×6
7.	1 ×4	2 ×5	1 ×6	9 ×3	7 ×3	4 ×6

Perfect score: 42   My score: _____

87

Problem Solving

Solve each problem.

1. There are 6 rows of cactus plants. Each row has 4 plants. How many cactus plants are there in all?

There are _____ rows of cactus plants.

There are _____ cactus plants in each row.

There are _____ cactus plants in all.

1.

2. There are 8 marigold plants in each row. There are 6 rows. How many marigold plants are there?

There are _____ marigold plants in each row.

There are _____ rows of marigold plants.

There are _____ marigold plants in all.

2.

3. There are 6 rose bushes in each row. There are 9 rows. How many rose bushes are there?

There are _____ rose bushes in each row.

There are _____ rows of rose bushes.

There are _____ rose bushes in all.

3.

Perfect score: 9   My score: _____

88

Lesson 2 Multiplication

$$\begin{array}{r} 4 \\ \times 7 \\ \hline \end{array} \qquad \begin{array}{r} 5 \\ \times 7 \\ \hline \end{array} \qquad \begin{array}{r} 6 \\ \times 7 \\ \hline \end{array} \qquad \begin{array}{r} 7 \\ \times 7 \\ \hline \end{array} \qquad \begin{array}{r} 8 \\ \times 7 \\ \hline \end{array} \qquad \begin{array}{r} 9 \\ \times 7 \\ \hline \end{array}$$

28   35   42

+7   +7   +7   +7   +7

$$\begin{array}{r} 4 \\ \times 8 \\ \hline \end{array} \qquad \begin{array}{r} 5 \\ \times 8 \\ \hline \end{array} \qquad \begin{array}{r} 6 \\ \times 8 \\ \hline \end{array} \qquad \begin{array}{r} 7 \\ \times 8 \\ \hline \end{array} \qquad \begin{array}{r} 8 \\ \times 8 \\ \hline \end{array} \qquad \begin{array}{r} 9 \\ \times 8 \\ \hline \end{array}$$

32   40   48

+8   +8   +8   +8   +8

Multiply.

	a	b	c	d	e	f
1.	7 ×7	7 ×6	6 ×8	3 ×7	9 ×8	0 ×7
2.	8 ×8	8 ×5	1 ×8	7 ×3	3 ×8	1 ×7
3.	8 ×0	8 ×6	5 ×8	9 ×7	7 ×1	6 ×7
4.	7 ×8	5 ×7	7 ×0	7 ×2	7 ×5	0 ×8
5.	8 ×7	2 ×8	8 ×4	7 ×4	8 ×3	4 ×8
6.	9 ×4	8 ×1	4 ×7	8 ×2	2 ×7	9 ×6

Perfect score: 36   My score: _____

Problem Solving

Solve each problem.

1. In Rita's building there are 7 floors. There are 9 apartments on each floor. How many apartments are in the building?

There are _____ floors in this building.

There are _____ apartments on each floor.

There are _____ apartments in Rita's building.

1.

2. The science club meets 4 times each month. The club meets for 7 months. How many meetings will the science club have?

The science club meets _____ times each month.

The club meets for _____ months.

The club will have _____ meetings in all.

2.

3. Each bag of corn weighs 8 kilograms. There are 7 bags. How much do the bags weigh in all?

Each bag weighs _____ kilograms.

There are _____ bags.

The bags weigh _____ kilograms in all.

3.

4. There are 7 days in a week. How many days are there in 5 weeks?

There are _____ days in 5 weeks.

4.

5.

5. Brenda walks 6 blocks each day going to and from school. How many blocks does she walk going to and from school in 7 days?

Brenda walks _____ blocks in 7 days.

Perfect score: 11   My score: _____

90

Lesson 3 Multiplication

9-column →

x	0	1	2	3	4	5	6	7	8	9
0	0	0	0	0	0	0	0	0	0	0
1	0	1	2	3	4	5	6	7	8	9
2	0	2	4	6	8	10	12	14	16	18
3	0	3	6	9	12	15	18	21	24	27
4	0	4	8	12	16	20	24	28	32	36
5	0	5	10	15	20	25	30	35	40	45
6	0	6	12	18	24	30	36	42	48	54
7	0	7	14	21	28	35	42	49	56	63
8	0	8	16	24	32	40	48	56	64	72
9	0	9	18	27	36	45	54	63	72	(81)

$$
\begin{array}{r}
9 \\
\times 9 \\
\hline
81
\end{array}
$$

9 → Find the 9 -row.

×9 → Find the 9 -column.

81 ← The product is named where the 9-row and 9-column meet.

9-row →

Multiply.

	a	b	c	d	e	f
1.	$\begin{array}{r} 7 \\ \times 9 \\ \hline \end{array}$	$\begin{array}{r} 9 \\ \times 6 \\ \hline \end{array}$	$\begin{array}{r} 8 \\ \times 8 \\ \hline \end{array}$	$\begin{array}{r} 3 \\ \times 7 \\ \hline \end{array}$	$\begin{array}{r} 2 \\ \times 9 \\ \hline \end{array}$	$\begin{array}{r} 7 \\ \times 3 \\ \hline \end{array}$
2.	$\begin{array}{r} 8 \\ \times 5 \\ \hline \end{array}$	$\begin{array}{r} 8 \\ \times 7 \\ \hline \end{array}$	$\begin{array}{r} 4 \\ \times 9 \\ \hline \end{array}$	$\begin{array}{r} 6 \\ \times 8 \\ \hline \end{array}$	$\begin{array}{r} 7 \\ \times 0 \\ \hline \end{array}$	$\begin{array}{r} 7 \\ \times 7 \\ \hline \end{array}$
3.	$\begin{array}{r} 9 \\ \times 9 \\ \hline \end{array}$	$\begin{array}{r} 1 \\ \times 8 \\ \hline \end{array}$	$\begin{array}{r} 0 \\ \times 9 \\ \hline \end{array}$	$\begin{array}{r} 6 \\ \times 9 \\ \hline \end{array}$	$\begin{array}{r} 7 \\ \times 8 \\ \hline \end{array}$	$\begin{array}{r} 2 \\ \times 8 \\ \hline \end{array}$
4.	$\begin{array}{r} 4 \\ \times 8 \\ \hline \end{array}$	$\begin{array}{r} 0 \\ \times 7 \\ \hline \end{array}$	$\begin{array}{r} 4 \\ \times 7 \\ \hline \end{array}$	$\begin{array}{r} 9 \\ \times 2 \\ \hline \end{array}$	$\begin{array}{r} 8 \\ \times 4 \\ \hline \end{array}$	$\begin{array}{r} 6 \\ \times 7 \\ \hline \end{array}$
5.	$\begin{array}{r} 5 \\ \times 8 \\ \hline \end{array}$	$\begin{array}{r} 9 \\ \times 7 \\ \hline \end{array}$	$\begin{array}{r} 3 \\ \times 8 \\ \hline \end{array}$	$\begin{array}{r} 1 \\ \times 9 \\ \hline \end{array}$	$\begin{array}{r} 1 \\ \times 7 \\ \hline \end{array}$	$\begin{array}{r} 0 \\ \times 8 \\ \hline \end{array}$
6.	$\begin{array}{r} 5 \\ \times 9 \\ \hline \end{array}$	$\begin{array}{r} 8 \\ \times 0 \\ \hline \end{array}$	$\begin{array}{r} 3 \\ \times 9 \\ \hline \end{array}$	$\begin{array}{r} 5 \\ \times 7 \\ \hline \end{array}$	$\begin{array}{r} 8 \\ \times 9 \\ \hline \end{array}$	$\begin{array}{r} 2 \\ \times 7 \\ \hline \end{array}$

Perfect score: 36   My score: _____

Problem Solving

Solve each problem.

1. There are 8 chairs around each table. There are 9 tables. How many chairs are around all the tables?

There are _____ chairs around each table.

There are _____ tables.

There are _____ chairs around all the tables.

2. Workers are eating lunch at 9 tables. Each table has 9 workers. How many workers are eating lunch?

There are _____ tables.

_____ workers are at each table.

_____ workers are eating lunch.

3. The workers drink 9 liters of milk each day. They are at work 5 days each week. How many liters of milk do they drink in 5 days?

They drink _____ liters of milk in 5 days.

4. A bowling league bowls 4 times each month. How many times will the league bowl in 9 months?

The bowling league will bowl _____ times.

5. There are 9 packages of golf balls. Each package has 6 golf balls. How many golf balls are there in all?

There are _____ golf balls.

6. A regular baseball game is 9 innings long. How many innings are in 7 regular games?

There are _____ innings in 7 regular games.

1.	
2.	
3.	**4.**
5.	**6.**

Perfect score: 10   My score: _____

92

Lesson 4   Multiplication

Multiply.

	a	b	c	d	e	f
1.	7 ×9	6 ×7	1 ×5	2 ×9	3 ×6	8 ×8
2.	3 ×7	4 ×9	0 ×8	7 ×5	7 ×8	6 ×6
3.	9 ×5	4 ×6	5 ×9	2 ×8	8 ×7	0 ×7
4.	7 ×6	1 ×6	9 ×8	0 ×9	5 ×5	9 ×7
5.	8 ×5	4 ×8	4 ×7	0 ×6	1 ×9	4 ×5
6.	6 ×8	9 ×6	6 ×5	6 ×4	7 ×7	3 ×9
7.	8 ×6	5 ×8	7 ×4	3 ×5	9 ×9	1 ×7
8.	9 ×4	5 ×7	1 ×8	8 ×9	5 ×6	2 ×5
9.	2 ×6	0 ×5	6 ×9	3 ×8	8 ×4	2 ×7

Perfect score: 54   My score: _____

Problem Solving

Solve each problem.

1. Some pupils formed 5 teams. There were 8 pupils on each team. How many pupils were there?

There were _____ teams.

There were _____ pupils on each team.

There were _____ pupils in all.

2. The waiter put 9 napkins on each table. There were 9 tables. How many napkins did the waiter use?

The waiter put _____ napkins on each table.

There were _____ tables.

The waiter used _____ napkins in all.

3. Dr. Mede rides her bicycle 6 kilometers every day. How far would she ride in 9 days?

Dr. Mede rides _____ kilometers every day.

She rides for each of _____ days.

She would ride _____ kilometers in all.

4. Mr. Brown works 7 hours each day. How many hours will he work in 6 days?

Mr. Brown will work _____ hours in 6 days.

5. There are 8 hot dogs in each package. How many hot dogs are there in 9 packages?

There are _____ hot dogs in 9 packages.

6. Suppose you read 8 stories every day. How many stories would you read in 7 days?

You would read _____ stories in 7 days.

1.	
2.	
3.	4.
5.	6.

Perfect score: 12   My score: _____

94

CHAPTER 8 TEST

NAME _____

Multiply.

	a	b	c	d	e
1.	6 ×7	5 ×9	8 ×6	4 ×7	7 ×7
2.	9 ×7	9 ×9	1 ×7	4 ×6	7 ×9
3.	0 ×6	7 ×8	5 ×8	9 ×8	7 ×6
4.	8 ×9	4 ×8	9 ×6	2 ×7	3 ×9

Solve each problem.

5. A clerk puts 6 oranges in each package. How many oranges are needed to make 9 packages?

There are _____ oranges in each package.

There are to be _____ packages.

_____ oranges are needed in all.

5.

6. A barbershop can handle 8 customers in one hour. How many customers can it handle in 8 hours?

It could handle _____ customers.

6.

7. Mr. Lawkin put 3 pictures in a row. He made 8 rows. How many pictures did he use?

Mr. Lawkin used _____ pictures.

7.

Perfect score: 25   My score: _____

PRE-TEST—Multiplication

Multiply.

	a	b	c	d	e	f
1.	3 ×2	3 0 ×2	2 ×4	2 0 ×4	1 ×7	1 0 ×7
2.	3 2 ×3	2 4 ×2	1 3 ×3	2 1 ×4	1 1 ×5	2 3 ×3
3.	7 ×4	7 0 ×4	6 ×3	6 0 ×3	9 ×4	9 0 ×4
4.	6 2 ×3	7 4 ×2	3 1 ×8	6 2 ×4	8 3 ×2	4 1 ×5
5.	1 8 ×4	2 6 ×3	3 5 ×2	2 4 ×3	3 8 ×2	1 6 ×5
6.	4 3 ×4	2 7 ×5	3 5 ×3	4 6 ×6	2 8 ×6	5 4 ×5
7.	5 6 ×7	6 3 ×2	8 0 ×5	2 3 ×2	3 7 ×2	4 5 ×5
8.	1 7 ×4	4 0 ×8	7 3 ×3	2 2 ×3	5 4 ×3	2 7 ×6
9.	3 0 ×9	5 8 ×4	2 8 ×4	2 5 ×3	8 0 ×4	6 6 ×2

Perfect score: 54   My score: _____

Lesson 1   Multiplication

```
   4        40         2        20    |      7        70         8        80
  ×2        ×2        ×3        ×3     |     ×3        ×3        ×4        ×4
  ───       ───       ───       ───   |     ───       ───       ───       ───
   8        80         6        60    |     21       210        32       320
```

Multiply.

	a	b	c	d	e	f

1.
```
   3        30         2        20         6        60
  ×2        ×2        ×4        ×4        ×1        ×1
  ───       ───       ───       ───       ───       ───
```

2.
```
  10        40        10        10        30        70
  ×8        ×2        ×9        ×3        ×3        ×1
  ───       ───       ───       ───       ───       ───
```

3.
```
   9        90         6        60         5        50
  ×4        ×4        ×3        ×3        ×5        ×5
  ───       ───       ───       ───       ───       ───
```

4.
```
  70        60        40        50        80        90
  ×3        ×5        ×4        ×2        ×3        ×6
  ───       ───       ───       ───       ───       ───
```

5.
```
  20        30        40        20        30        40
  ×4        ×5        ×3        ×2        ×6        ×7
  ───       ───       ───       ───       ───       ───
```

6.
```
  70        30        10        80        90        60
  ×7        ×8        ×7        ×8        ×1        ×4
  ───       ───       ───       ───       ───       ───
```

7.
```
  40        20        60        50        10        40
  ×5        ×8        ×2        ×3        ×5        ×1
  ───       ───       ───       ───       ───       ───
```

8.
```
  60        50        80        20        70        90
  ×7        ×5        ×3        ×9        ×8        ×3
  ───       ───       ───       ───       ───       ───
```

Perfect score: 48   My score: _____

Problem Solving

Solve each problem.

1. There are 4 classrooms on the first floor. Each classroom has 30 seats. How many seats are on the first floor?

_____ seats are in each classroom.

_____ classrooms are on the first floor.

_____ seats are on the first floor.

2. Laura placed 2 boxes on a wagon. Each box weighs 20 kilograms. How much do the two boxes weigh?

Each box weighs _____ kilograms.

Laura placed _____ boxes on the wagon.

The two boxes weigh _____ kilograms.

3. Terry bought 3 packages of paper. Each package had 30 sheets. How many sheets of paper did he buy?

Each package contains _____ sheets of paper.

Terry bought _____ packages of paper.

Terry bought _____ sheets of paper.

4. Mrs. Long bought 6 boxes of nails. Each box had 30 nails. How many nails did she buy?

Mrs. Long bought _____ nails.

5. There are 40 bottles in a case. How many bottles are there in 2 cases?

There are _____ bottles in 2 cases.

6. A bus has 40 passenger seats. How many passenger seats would there be on 7 such buses?

There are _____ passenger seats on 7 buses.

1.	
2.	
3.	4.
5.	6.

Perfect score: 12   My score: _____

98

Lesson 2   Multiplication

	Multiply 2 ones by 3.	Multiply 7 tens by 3.	

```
   72          72          72          72
  ×3          ×3          ×3          ×3
  ——          ——          ——          ——
               6           6           6  ⎫
                          210         210 ⎬ Add.
                                      ———  ⎭
                                      216
```

Multiply.

	a	*b*	*c*	*d*	*e*	*f*
1.	6 2 ×2	7 3 ×3	9 2 ×4	8 4 ×2	5 3 ×2	4 2 ×3
2.	2 3 ×2	3 1 ×3	4 2 ×2	1 2 ×4	3 3 ×3	4 2 ×2
3.	2 1 ×4	6 1 ×3	5 1 ×2	4 3 ×2	8 2 ×4	1 3 ×3
4.	7 2 ×3	3 2 ×3	4 3 ×3	2 3 ×3	3 4 ×2	9 3 ×2

Perfect score: 24   My score: _____

Lesson 3   Multiplication

	Multiply 4 ones by 2.	Multiply. 8 tens by 2.
84 ×2	84 ×2 —— 8	84 ×2 —— 168

Multiply.

	a	b	c	d	e	f
1.	6 2 ×4	8 4 ×2	7 3 ×3	8 2 ×2	9 1 ×2	5 2 ×3
2.	4 3 ×2	4 1 ×4	3 2 ×3	6 1 ×3	4 2 ×4	4 4 ×2
3.	7 2 ×3	7 1 ×3	8 1 ×2	4 3 ×3	5 2 ×4	8 3 ×2
4.	6 2 ×2	9 3 ×3	5 2 ×1	7 4 ×2	5 3 ×2	6 2 ×3
5.	7 2 ×4	8 1 ×5	9 2 ×3	6 3 ×3	5 4 ×2	7 3 ×2
6.	6 1 ×7	3 2 ×4	8 2 ×3	8 1 ×9	6 3 ×2	9 1 ×5
7.	5 3 ×3	7 1 ×6	8 2 ×4	9 1 ×9	9 2 ×4	8 1 ×8

Perfect score: 42   My score: _____

Lesson 4   Multiplication

Multiply
7 ones by 3.

Multiply 1 ten by 3.
Add the 2 tens.

$$17 \atop \times 3$$

$$\begin{array}{r} \overset{2}{17} \\ \times 3 \\ \hline 1 \end{array}$$

$3 \times 7 = 21 = 20 + 1$

$3 \times 10 = 30$

$$\begin{array}{r} \overset{2}{17} \\ \times 3 \\ \hline 51 \end{array}$$

$30 + 20 = 50$

$$\begin{array}{r} 17 \\ \times 3 \\ \hline 51 \end{array}$$

Multiply.

	a	b	c	d	e	f
1.	2 3 ×4	2 9 ×3	1 6 ×5	1 4 ×7	2 6 ×3	1 2 ×8
2.	3 7 ×2	2 6 ×2	4 7 ×2	2 8 ×3	1 5 ×5	2 4 ×4
3.	1 8 ×5	1 4 ×5	2 8 ×3	3 5 ×2	4 6 ×2	3 8 ×2
4.	4 5 ×2	2 7 ×3	1 5 ×6	1 2 ×7	1 5 ×4	4 8 ×2
5.	2 8 ×2	1 2 ×6	1 7 ×5	1 3 ×6	1 9 ×3	1 9 ×4
6.	3 6 ×2	2 4 ×3	2 5 ×3	1 6 ×4	2 9 ×2	1 8 ×3

Perfect score: 36   My score: _____

Problem Solving

Solve each problem.

1. Ms. McClean ordered 7 dozen radio antennas. How many antennas did she order? (There are 12 items in a dozen.)

There are _____ items in a dozen.

She ordered _____ dozen antennas.

Ms. McClean ordered _____ radio antennas.

2. There are 14 CB radio units on a shelf. Each unit weighs 5 kilograms. How much do all the units weigh?

There are _____ radio units.

Each unit weighs _____ kilograms.

All the units weigh _____ kilograms.

3. Mr. Tunin bought 2 CB radio units. Each unit cost $49. How much did both units cost?

Both units cost $ _____.

4. Ms. McClean sold 36 radios this week. She sold the same number of radios last week. How many radios did she sell in the two weeks?

She sold _____ radios in the two weeks.

1.

2.

3.

4.

Perfect score: 8   My score: _____

Lesson 5   Multiplication

Multiply
7 ones by 5.

Multiply 5 tens by 5.
Add the 3 tens.

$$57$$
$$\times 5$$

$$\begin{array}{r} ^{3}\\ 57 \\ \times 5 \\ \hline 5 \end{array}$$

$5 \times 7 = 35 = 30 + 5$

$5 \times 50 = 250$

$$\begin{array}{r} ^{3}\\ 57 \\ \times 5 \\ \hline 285 \end{array}$$

$250 + 30 = 280 = 200 + 80$

Multiply.

	a	b	c	d	e	f
1.	3 5 ×4	4 2 ×6	5 6 ×3	4 7 ×5	3 8 ×6	2 5 ×5
2.	5 4 ×4	2 7 ×6	3 8 ×5	4 8 ×8	8 3 ×7	7 4 ×6
3.	7 5 ×4	5 8 ×3	4 6 ×4	3 7 ×6	2 9 ×5	4 6 ×3
4.	8 4 ×4	9 3 ×6	6 2 ×8	5 7 ×5	3 9 ×4	2 2 ×7
5.	4 5 ×6	6 8 ×7	7 3 ×9	8 7 ×8	9 4 ×6	8 3 ×4
6.	9 6 ×5	8 5 ×3	4 7 ×4	2 3 ×9	3 9 ×7	6 5 ×6

Perfect score: 36   My score: _____

Problem Solving

Solve each problem.

1. Ernest's spelling book has 25 new words on each page. There are 9 pages in the first section. How many new words are there in the first section?

There are _____ new spelling words on each page.

There are _____ pages in the first section.

There are _____ new spelling words in the first section.

2. Alan wants to walk up 6 flights of stairs. There are 26 steps in each flight. How many steps will he have to walk up?

There are _____ steps in each flight.

Alan wants to walk up _____ flights.

Alan will have to walk up _____ steps.

3. There are 7 rows of seats in the balcony. There are 36 seats in each row. How many seats are in the balcony?

There are _____ seats in each row.

There are _____ rows.

There are _____ seats in the balcony.

4. There are 25 baseball players on each team. How many players are there on 8 such teams?

There are _____ players on 8 teams.

5. Bev used 3 rolls of film. She took 36 pictures on each roll. How many pictures did Bev take?

Bev took _____ pictures.

1.

2.

3.

4.   5.

Perfect score: 11   My score: _____

104

CHAPTER 9 TEST

Multiply.

	a	*b*	*c*	*d*	*e*
1.	3 0 ×2	4 2 ×2	2 3 ×3	6 0 ×4	8 0 ×3
2.	8 4 ×2	7 3 ×3	2 1 ×7	1 4 ×6	2 7 ×3
3.	5 7 ×5	3 8 ×6	4 2 ×5	2 9 ×4	3 6 ×5
4.	1 5 ×4	7 3 ×2	5 8 ×3	4 0 ×9	2 8 ×3

Solve each problem.

5. Mary has 4 decks of cards. There are 52 cards in each deck. How many cards does she have?

She has _____ decks.

There are _____ cards in each deck.

Mary has _____ cards in all.

5.

6. Tom's father works 37 hours each week. How many hours would he work in 4 weeks?

He would work _____ hours in 4 weeks.

7. Mr. Richards gave each pupil 3 sheets of paper. There were 28 pupils. How many sheets of paper did he use?

Mr. Richards used _____ sheets of paper.

6.

7.

Perfect score: 25   My score: _____

PRE-TEST—Division

Divide.

	a	*b*	*c*	*d*	*e*
1.	2⟌6	2⟌1 2	2⟌1 8	2⟌4	2⟌1 0
2.	4⟌1 6	3⟌2 4	3⟌9	5⟌2 5	3⟌3
3.	1⟌4	1⟌8	1⟌1 6	4⟌3 6	1⟌2 7
4.	2⟌1 6	1⟌1	3⟌2 7	1⟌6	1⟌2 1
5.	1⟌1 2	5⟌2 0	2⟌1 4	4⟌8	1⟌1 4
6.	1⟌5	4⟌2 8	5⟌5	1⟌2	3⟌1 8

Solve each problem.

7. Paula has 18 books. She put them in piles of 3 books each. How many piles of books does she have?

She has _____ piles of books.

7.

8. Jake has 12 pennies. He put 3 pennies in each stack. How many stacks of pennies does he have?

He has _____ stacks of pennies.

8.

9. Dee has 12 pennies. She put 2 pennies in each stack. How many stacks of pennies does she have?

She has _____ stacks of pennies.

9.

Perfect score: 33   My score: _____

Lesson 1   Division

÷ and $\overline{\smash{\big)}}$ mean divide.

6 ÷ 2 = 3 is read "6 divided by 2 is equal to 3."

8 ÷ 2 = 4 is read "_____ divided by 2 is equal to _____."

$2\overline{\smash{\big)}6}$ is read "6 divided by 2 is equal to 3."

$\overset{4}{2\overline{\smash{\big)}8}}$ is read "_____ divided by 2 is equal to _____."

divisor - - - - → $2\overset{3 \;\text{← - - - quotient}}{\overline{\smash{\big)}6} \;\text{← - - - dividend}}$

In $2\overline{\smash{\big)}8}^{\,4}$, the divisor is _____, the dividend is _____, and the quotient is _____.

Complete each sentence.

1.   10 ÷ 2 = 5 is read "_____ divided by 2 is equal to _____."

2.   21 ÷ 3 = 7 is read "_____ divided by 3 is equal to _____."

3.   4 ÷ 2 = 2 is read "_____ divided by 2 is equal to _____."

4. $3\overline{\smash{\big)}18}^{\,6}$ is read "_____ divided by 3 is equal to _____."

5. $2\overline{\smash{\big)}18}^{\,9}$ is read "_____ divided by 2 is equal to _____."

6. $3\overline{\smash{\big)}24}^{\,8}$ is read "_____ divided by 3 is equal to _____."

7.   In $3\overline{\smash{\big)}21}^{\,7}$, the divisor is _____, the dividend is _____, and the quotient is _____.

8.   In $2\overline{\smash{\big)}4}^{\,2}$, the divisor is _____, the dividend is _____, and the quotient is _____.

9.   In $2\overline{\smash{\big)}10}^{\,5}$, the divisor is _____, the dividend is _____, and the quotient is _____.

10. In $3\overline{\smash{\big)}18}^{\,6}$, the divisor is _____, the dividend is _____, and the quotient is _____.

Perfect score: 24   My score: _____

Lesson 2   Division

NAME _____

6 ✕'s in all.
2 ✕'s in each group.
How many groups?

6 ÷ 2 = _3_

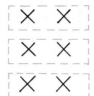

There are _3_ groups.

6 ✕'s in all.
3 groups of ✕'s.
How many ✕'s in each group?

6 ÷ 3 = ____

There are ____ ✕'s in each group.

Complete the following.

a

b

1. 10 ☆'s in all.
2 ☆'s in each group.
How many groups?

10 ÷ 2 = ____

There are ____ groups.

10 ☆'s in all.
5 groups of ☆'s.
How many ☆'s in each group?

10 ÷ 5 = ____

There are ____ ☆'s in each group.

2. 8 ☐'s in all.

____ ☐'s in each group.
How many groups?

8 ÷ 2 = ____

There are ____ groups.

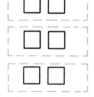

____ ☐'s in all.

4 groups of ☐'s.
How many ☐'s in each group?

8 ÷ 4 = ____

There are ____ ☐'s in each group.

3. ____ ◯'s in all.

____ ◯'s in each group.
How many groups?

4 ÷ 2 = ____

There are ____ groups.

____ ◯'s in all.

____ groups of ◯'s.
How many ◯'s in each group?

4 ÷ 2 = ____

There are ____ ◯'s in each group.

Perfect score: 18   My score: _____

108

Lesson 3   Division

```
3 -----→ 3
×2 ----→ 2�罫6
6 --------⌐
```

```
4 -----→ 4
×3 ----→ 3⎲12
12 --------⌐
```

If $2 \times 3 = 6$, then $6 \div 2 = 3$.   If $3 \times 4 = 12$, then $12 \div 3 = 4$.

Divide as shown.

	a		*b*	

1.
```
    5
   ×2        2⎲1 0
   10
```
```
    6
   ×3        3⎲1 8
   18
```

2.
```
    7
   ×2        2⎲1 4
   14
```
```
    8
   ×3        3⎲2 4
   24
```

3.
```
    1
   ×2        2⎲2
    2
```
```
    3
   ×3        3⎲9
    9
```

4.
```
    8
   ×2        2⎲1 6
   16
```
```
    9
   ×3        3⎲2 7
   27
```

Divide.

	a	*b*	*c*	*d*

5.   3⎲1 5   2⎲6   3⎲3   3⎲6

6.   3⎲2 1   2⎲1 8   2⎲8   2⎲1 2

Perfect score: 16   My score: _____

Problem Solving

Solve each problem.

1. Twenty-four people are at work. They work in 3 departments. The same number of people work in each department. How many people work in each department?

There are _____ people.

They work in _____ departments.

There are _____ people in each department.

2. Dan put 8 books into 2 stacks. Each stack had the same number of books. How many books were in each stack?

There were _____ books in all.

They were put into _____ stacks.

There were _____ books in each stack.

3. Janice put 16 liters of water into 2 jars. She put the same number of liters into each jar. How many liters of water did she put into each jar?

Janice put _____ liters of water into jars.

She used _____ jars.

Janice put _____ liters of water into each jar.

4. Kim has 27 apples. She wants to put the same number of apples in each of 3 boxes. How many apples should she put in each box?

She should put _____ apples in each box.

5. Mr. Green had 18 inches of wire. He cut the wire into 2 pieces. The pieces were the same length. How long was each piece?

Each piece was _____ inches long.

1.

2.

3.

4.

5.

Perfect score: 11   My score: _____

110

Lesson 4   Division

$$
\begin{array}{c}
5 \\
\times 4 \\
\hline
20
\end{array}
\quad \longrightarrow \quad
4\overline{)20}
\qquad\qquad
\begin{array}{c}
9 \\
\times 5 \\
\hline
45
\end{array}
\quad \longrightarrow \quad
5\overline{)45}
$$

If $4 \times 5 = 20$, then $20 \div 4 = 5$.   If $5 \times 9 = 45$, then _____ $\div 5 =$ _____.

Divide as shown.

	a			b	

1.
$$
\begin{array}{c} 7 \\ \times 4 \\ \hline 28 \end{array}
\qquad 4\overline{)28}
\qquad\qquad
\begin{array}{c} 6 \\ \times 5 \\ \hline 30 \end{array}
\qquad 5\overline{)30}
$$

2.
$$
\begin{array}{c} 4 \\ \times 4 \\ \hline 16 \end{array}
\qquad 4\overline{)16}
\qquad\qquad
\begin{array}{c} 3 \\ \times 5 \\ \hline 15 \end{array}
\qquad 5\overline{)15}
$$

3.
$$
\begin{array}{c} 6 \\ \times 4 \\ \hline 24 \end{array}
\qquad 4\overline{)24}
\qquad\qquad
\begin{array}{c} 4 \\ \times 5 \\ \hline 20 \end{array}
\qquad 5\overline{)20}
$$

4.
$$
\begin{array}{c} 9 \\ \times 4 \\ \hline 36 \end{array}
\qquad 4\overline{)36}
\qquad\qquad
\begin{array}{c} 8 \\ \times 5 \\ \hline 40 \end{array}
\qquad 5\overline{)40}
$$

Divide.

a	b	c	d

5. $4\overline{)8}$ $5\overline{)10}$ $4\overline{)4}$ $4\overline{)12}$

6. $5\overline{)25}$ $5\overline{)5}$ $4\overline{)32}$ $5\overline{)35}$

Perfect score: 15   My score: _____

Problem Solving

Solve each problem.

1. A loaf of bread has 24 slices. Mrs. Spencer uses 4 slices each day. How long will a loaf of bread last her?

A loaf of bread has _____ slices.

Mrs. Spencer uses _____ slices a day.

The loaf of bread will last _____ days.

2. A football team played 28 periods. There are 4 periods in a game. How many games did they play?

The football team played _____ periods.

There are _____ periods each game.

The football team played _____ games.

3. A basketball game is 32 minutes long. The game is separated into 4 parts. Each part has the same number of minutes. How long is each part?

A basketball game is _____ minutes long.

The game is separated into _____ parts.

Each part is _____ minutes long.

4. Lilly worked 25 problems. She worked 5 problems on each sheet of paper. How many sheets of paper did she use?

She used _____ sheets of paper.

5. Robert works the same number of hours each week. He worked 45 hours in 5 weeks. How many hours does he work each week?

Robert works _____ hours each week.

1.
2.
3.
4.
5.

Perfect score: 11   My score: _____

Lesson 5 Division

```
   8 -----→  8
  ×1 ----→ 1⟌8
   8 ------→↑
```

```
  15 ----→ 15
  ×1 ---→ 1⟌15
  15 -----→↑
```

If $1 \times 8 = 8$, then $8 \div 1 = 8$. | If $1 \times 15 = 15$, then _____ $\div 1 =$ _____.

Divide.

	a			*b*	
1.	5 ×1 — 5	1⟌5		14 ×1 — 14	1⟌1 4
2.	4 ×1 — 4	1⟌4		9 ×1 — 9	1⟌9

	a	*b*	*c*	*d*	*e*
3.	1⟌4	1⟌3	1⟌1 2	1⟌2	1⟌1 6
4.	2⟌8	3⟌1 8	2⟌1 8	2⟌6	3⟌6
5.	4⟌1 6	2⟌1 4	1⟌9	5⟌5	5⟌4 5
6.	2⟌1 6	4⟌1 2	2⟌1 0	4⟌2 8	1⟌1 8
7.	4⟌4	4⟌2 0	5⟌1 0	5⟌3 0	4⟌3 2

Perfect score: 29   My score: _____

113

Problem Solving

Solve each problem.

1. Flo bought 16 rolls. The rolls came in 2 packs. The same number of rolls were in each pack. How many rolls were in each pack?

Flo bought _____ rolls.

These rolls filled _____ packs.

There were _____ rolls in each pack.

2. There are 9 families in an apartment building. There are 3 families on each floor. How many floors are in the building?

There are _____ families in the building.

There are _____ families on each floor.

There are _____ floors in the building.

3. Arlene put 36 oranges in bags. She put 4 oranges in each bag. How many bags did she fill?

Arlene put _____ oranges in bags.

She put _____ oranges in each bag.

Arlene filled _____ bags with oranges.

4. Marcos read 35 pages of science in 5 days. He read the same number of pages each day. How many pages did he read each day?

Marcos read _____ pages each day.

5. Mrs. Allan worked 25 hours in 5 days. She worked the same number of hours each day. How many hours did she work each day?

Mrs. Allan worked _____ hours each day.

1.

2.

3.

4.

5.

Perfect score: 11   My score: _____

114

CHAPTER 10 TEST

Divide.

	a	*b*	*c*	*d*	*e*

1. $2\overline{)10}$ $1\overline{)4}$ $3\overline{)3}$ $3\overline{)9}$ $2\overline{)16}$

2. $1\overline{)12}$ $2\overline{)12}$ $3\overline{)12}$ $2\overline{)14}$ $3\overline{)15}$

3. $3\overline{)6}$ $1\overline{)8}$ $5\overline{)20}$ $1\overline{)9}$ $3\overline{)24}$

4. $5\overline{)40}$ $5\overline{)5}$ $1\overline{)10}$ $4\overline{)36}$ $4\overline{)24}$

Solve each problem.

5. The 45 pupils in a class separated into 5 groups. Each group has the same number of pupils. How many are in each group?

There are _____ pupils in all.

The pupils are separated into _____ groups.

There are _____ pupils in each group.

5.

6. Shirley has 28 balloons for a party. She will give each person 4 balloons. How many people will receive balloons?

_____ people will receive balloons.

6.

7. Mr. Graham has 6 birds. How many cages does he need in order to put 2 birds in each cage?

Mr. Graham needs _____ cages.

7.

Perfect score: 25   My score: _____

PRE-TEST—Division

NAME _____

Chapter 11

Divide.

	a	b	c	d	e
1.	6⟌2 4	6⟌1 2	6⟌1 8	6⟌0	6⟌6
2.	6⟌4 2	6⟌5 4	6⟌3 0	6⟌3 6	6⟌4 8
3.	7⟌0	7⟌2 8	7⟌1 4	7⟌2 1	7⟌7
4.	7⟌5 6	7⟌4 2	7⟌6 3	7⟌3 5	7⟌4 9
5.	8⟌8	8⟌4 0	8⟌0	8⟌3 2	8⟌1 6
6.	8⟌2 4	8⟌4 8	8⟌6 4	8⟌7 2	8⟌5 6
7.	9⟌3 6	9⟌2 7	9⟌4 5	9⟌1 8	9⟌0
8.	9⟌7 2	9⟌6 3	9⟌5 4	9⟌9	9⟌8 1
9.	5⟌5	4⟌2 8	1⟌1	5⟌3 0	4⟌1 2

Perfect score: 45   My score: _____

116

Lesson 1   Division

$$3 \quad \cdots\cdots\rightarrow \quad 3$$
$$\times 6 \quad \cdots\rightarrow \quad 6\overline{)18}$$
$$\overline{18} \quad \cdots\cdots\cdots\rightarrow$$

$$4 \quad \cdots\cdots\rightarrow \quad 4$$
$$\times 6 \quad \cdots\rightarrow \quad 6\overline{)24}$$
$$\overline{24} \quad \cdots\cdots\cdots\rightarrow$$

If $6 \times 3 = 18$, then $18 \div 6 = 3$.

If $6 \times 4 = 24$, then _____ $\div 6 =$ _____.

Divide.

	a		*b*	
1.	$\begin{array}{r} 2 \\ \times 6 \\ \hline 12 \end{array}$	$6\overline{)1\ 2}$	$\begin{array}{r} 1 \\ \times 6 \\ \hline 6 \end{array}$	$6\overline{)6}$
2.	$\begin{array}{r} 5 \\ \times 6 \\ \hline 30 \end{array}$	$6\overline{)3\ 0}$	$\begin{array}{r} 7 \\ \times 6 \\ \hline 42 \end{array}$	$6\overline{)4\ 2}$
3.	$\begin{array}{r} 8 \\ \times 6 \\ \hline 48 \end{array}$	$6\overline{)4\ 8}$	$\begin{array}{r} 9 \\ \times 6 \\ \hline 54 \end{array}$	$6\overline{)5\ 4}$

	a	*b*	*c*	*d*
4.	$6\overline{)6}$	$6\overline{)1\ 2}$	$6\overline{)3\ 6}$	$6\overline{)1\ 8}$
5.	$1\overline{)6}$	$6\overline{)0}$	$6\overline{)2\ 4}$	$6\overline{)4\ 2}$
6.	$6\overline{)3\ 0}$	$6\overline{)5\ 4}$	$6\overline{)4\ 8}$	$5\overline{)4\ 5}$
7.	$4\overline{)3\ 2}$	$5\overline{)2\ 0}$	$4\overline{)2\ 0}$	$5\overline{)3\ 0}$

Perfect score: 22   My score: _____

Problem Solving

Solve each problem.

1. There are 6 rows of mailboxes. Each row has the same number of mailboxes. There are 30 mailboxes in all. How many are in each row?

There are _____ mailboxes in all.

The mailboxes are separated into _____ rows.

There are _____ mailboxes in each row.

2. The movie was shown 12 times in 6 days. It was shown the same number of times each day. How many times was it shown each day?

The movie was shown _____ times in all.

The movie was shown for _____ days.

The movie was shown _____ times each day.

3. Jill bought 18 buttons. The buttons were on cards of 6 buttons each. How many cards were there?

Jill bought _____ buttons.

There were _____ buttons on a card.

There were _____ cards.

4. Marvin got 6 hits in 6 games. He got the same number of hits in each game. How many hits did he get in each game?

Marvin got _____ hits in each game.

5. One side of a building has 24 windows. Each floor has 6 windows on that side. How many floors does the building have?

The building has _____ floors.

1.

2.

3.

4.

5.

Perfect score: 11   My score: _____

118

Lesson 2   Division

```
  3 - - - - →  3
 ×7 - - - → 7)21
 ──                              
  21 - - - - - ┘
```

```
  5 - - - - →  5
 ×8 - - - → 8)40
 ──
  40 - - - - - ┘
```

If $7 \times 3 = 21$, then $21 \div 7 = 3$.

If $8 \times 5 = 40$, then _____ $\div 8 =$ _____.

Divide.

a b

1.
```
   2
  ×7        7)1 4
  ──
  14
```
```
   3
  ×8        8)2 4
  ──
  24
```

2.
```
   5
  ×7        7)3 5
  ──
  35
```
```
   4
  ×8        8)3 2
  ──
  32
```

3.
```
   7
  ×7        7)4 9
  ──
  49
```
```
   8
  ×8        8)6 4
  ──
  64
```

a b c d

4. $7)\overline{7}$ $8)\overline{0}$ $8)\overline{1\ 6}$ $7)\overline{2\ 8}$

5. $8)\overline{4\ 8}$ $7)\overline{4\ 2}$ $8)\overline{8}$ $7)\overline{5\ 6}$

6. $7)\overline{0}$ $8)\overline{5\ 6}$ $1)\overline{7}$ $7)\overline{6\ 3}$

7. $1)\overline{8}$ $8)\overline{4\ 0}$ $8)\overline{7\ 2}$ $7)\overline{2\ 1}$

Perfect score: 22   My score: _____

Problem Solving

Solve each problem.

1. A classroom has 28 chairs in 7 rows. Each row has the same number of chairs. How many chairs are in each row?

There are _____ chairs in the classroom.

The chairs are separated into _____ rows.

There are _____ chairs in each row.

2. There are 48 chairs around the tables in the library. There are 8 chairs for each table. How many tables are in the library?

There are _____ chairs in the library.

There are _____ chairs around each table.

There are _____ tables in the library.

3. David worked the same number of hours each day. He worked 21 hours in 7 days. How many hours did he work each day?

David worked _____ hours each day.

4. There are 16 cars in the parking lot. There are 8 cars in each row. How many rows of cars are there?

There are _____ rows of cars.

5. Mr. Miller sold 7 cars in 7 days. He sold the same number of cars each day. How many did he sell each day?

Mr. Miller sold _____ car each day.

1.

2.

3.

4.

5.

Perfect score: 9   My score: _____

120

Lesson 3   Division

$$\begin{array}{r}2 \\ \times 9 \\ \hline 18\end{array} \longrightarrow 9\overline{\smash{)}18}$$

If $9 \times 2 = 18$, then $18 \div 9 = 2$.

$$\begin{array}{r}7 \\ \times 9 \\ \hline 63\end{array} \longrightarrow 9\overline{\smash{)}63}$$

If $9 \times 7 = 63$, then _____ $\div 9 =$ _____.

Divide.

	a		*b*	

1.
$$\begin{array}{r}5 \\ \times 9 \\ \hline 45\end{array} \qquad 9\overline{\smash{)}4\ 5} \qquad\qquad \begin{array}{r}3 \\ \times 9 \\ \hline 27\end{array} \qquad 9\overline{\smash{)}2\ 7}$$

2.
$$\begin{array}{r}8 \\ \times 9 \\ \hline 72\end{array} \qquad 9\overline{\smash{)}7\ 2} \qquad\qquad \begin{array}{r}4 \\ \times 9 \\ \hline 36\end{array} \qquad 9\overline{\smash{)}3\ 6}$$

3.
$$\begin{array}{r}6 \\ \times 9 \\ \hline 54\end{array} \qquad 9\overline{\smash{)}5\ 4} \qquad\qquad \begin{array}{r}9 \\ \times 9 \\ \hline 81\end{array} \qquad 9\overline{\smash{)}8\ 1}$$

	a	*b*	*c*	*d*
4.	$9\overline{\smash{)}9}$	$1\overline{\smash{)}9}$	$9\overline{\smash{)}1\ 8}$	$9\overline{\smash{)}3\ 6}$
5.	$9\overline{\smash{)}0}$	$9\overline{\smash{)}7\ 2}$	$9\overline{\smash{)}5\ 4}$	$9\overline{\smash{)}8\ 1}$
6.	$8\overline{\smash{)}7\ 2}$	$9\overline{\smash{)}6\ 3}$	$8\overline{\smash{)}4\ 8}$	$9\overline{\smash{)}4\ 5}$
7.	$9\overline{\smash{)}2\ 7}$	$8\overline{\smash{)}5\ 6}$	$7\overline{\smash{)}6\ 3}$	$7\overline{\smash{)}4\ 9}$

Perfect score: 22   My score: _____

Problem Solving

Solve each problem.

1. A farmer planted 54 cherry trees in 9 rows. Each row had the same number of trees. How many trees were in each row?

A farmer planted _____ trees.

There were _____ rows of trees.

There were _____ trees in each row.

2. Ray put 27 tennis balls in 9 cans. He put the same number of balls in each can. How many balls did Ray put in each can?

Ray put _____ tennis balls in cans.

There were _____ cans.

He put _____ balls in each can.

3. There are 9 packs of flashcubes on a shelf. Each pack has the same number of cubes. There are 36 flashcubes in all. How many cubes are in each pack?

There are _____ cubes in each pack.

4. There are 18 cornstalks in a garden. There are 9 stalks in each row. How many rows of cornstalks are there?

There are _____ rows of cornstalks.

5. Kay had 45 pennies. She put the pennies into stacks of 9 pennies each. How many stacks of pennies did she make?

She made _____ stacks of pennies.

1.	
2.	
3.	
4.	
5.	

Perfect score: 9   My score: _____

122

Lesson 4   Division

Divide.

	a	b	c	d
1.	2)1 0	3)1 8	4)4	1)8
2.	5)1 5	8)1 6	6)2 4	7)4 2
3.	2)1 8	3)2 4	7)3 5	9)0
4.	5)2 5	4)3 2	9)2 7	6)3 6
5.	7)1 4	3)1 5	8)8	2)1 6
6.	9)1 8	6)1 2	3)1 2	8)2 4
7.	5)2 0	4)1 2	2)6	5)1 0
8.	7)5 6	3)2 1	8)4 0	6)3 0
9.	4)2 8	9)4 5	7)4 9	9)7 2
10.	8)6 4	9)5 4	8)4 8	9)8 1

Perfect score: 40   My score: _____

Problem Solving

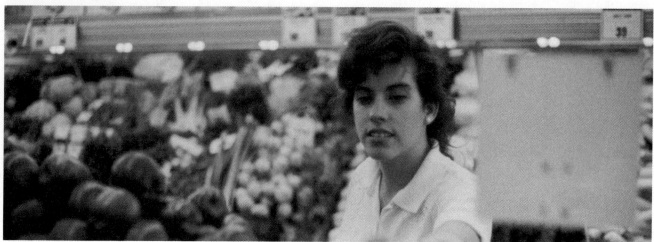

Solve each problem.

1. Marilyn has 42 apples. She puts 6 apples in a package. How many packages will she have?

Marilyn has _____ apples.

She puts _____ apples in each package.

There will be _____ packages of apples.

2. Marilyn has 63 peaches. She puts 7 peaches in a package. How many packages will she have?

Marilyn has _____ peaches.

Each package will have _____ peaches.

There will be _____ packages of peaches.

3. There are 8 packages of pears. Each package has the same number of pears. There are 64 pears in all. How many pears are in each package?

There are _____ pears in all.

There are _____ packages of pears.

There are _____ pears in each package.

1.

2.

3.

Perfect score: 9   My score: _____

CHAPTER 11 TEST

Divide.

	a	*b*	*c*	*d*	*e*
1.	6〉1 2	7〉7	8〉2 4	6〉3 6	9〉0
2.	7〉1 4	9〉4 5	6〉4 2	8〉3 2	1〉9
3.	6〉4 8	7〉2 1	8〉4 0	9〉1 8	8〉7 2
4.	8〉6 4	9〉8 1	7〉5 6	6〉5 4	6〉1 8
5.	6〉3 0	7〉2 8	9〉7 2	7〉6 3	8〉4 8

Solve each problem.

6. A classroom has 24 desks. They are in 6 rows. There is the same number of desks in each row. How many desks are in each row?

6.

There are _____ desks in all.

There are _____ rows with the same number of desks in each row.

There are _____ desks in each row.

7. Ted put 24 biscuits on a tray. He put 8 biscuits in each row. How many rows were there?

7.

There were _____ rows.

Perfect score: 29   My score: _____

PRE-TEST—Metric Measurement

Find the length of each object to the nearest centimeter.

1. _____ centimeters

2. _____ centimeters

3. _____ centimeters

4. _____ centimeters

5. _____ centimeters   ————————————

Answer *True* or *False*.

6. A liter is less than 800 milliliters.   _____

7. A liter is more than 1,800 milliliters.   _____

8. A liter is equal to 1,000 milliliters.   _____

Solve.

9. A car can go 6 kilometers on a liter of gasoline. The car has a tank that holds 55 liters. How far can the car go on a full tank of gasoline?

The car can go _____ kilometers.

Perfect score: 9   My score: _____

Lesson 1   Centimeter

1 centimeter or 1 cm

7 centimeters or 7 cm

_____ cm

Guess how long each object is in centimeters.
Then find the length of each object to the nearest centimeter.

1. Guess: _____ cm

Length: _____ cm

2. Guess: _____ cm

Length: _____ cm

3. Guess: _____ cm

Length: _____ cm

4. Guess: _____ cm

Length: _____ cm

5. Guess: _____ cm

Length: _____ cm

6. Guess: _____ cm

Length: _____ cm

Perfect score: 6   My score: _____

Problem Solving

Solve each problem.

1. Find the length of this book to the nearest centimeter.

It is _____ centimeters long.

2. Find the width of this book to the nearest centimeter.

It is _____ centimeters wide.

3. This book is how much longer than it is wide?

It is _____ centimeters longer than it is wide.

4. How many centimeters is it across a nickel?

It is _____ centimeters across.

5. How many centimeters would it be across 8 nickels laid in a row?

It would be _____ centimeters across.

6. Find the length of your shoe to the nearest centimeter.

It is _____ centimeters long.

Use a tape measure or string to find the following to the nearest centimeter.

7. the distance around your wrist _____ centimeters

8. the distance around your waist _____ centimeters

9. the distance around your head _____ centimeters

10. the distance around your ankle _____ centimeters

Perfect score: 10   My score: _____

128

Lesson 2   Metric Measurement

From A to B is a length of 12 centimeters.

Draw from C to D. It is _____ centimeters long.

---

1. Draw from E to F.

The length is _____ centimeters.

2. Draw from G to H.

The length is _____ centimeters.

3. Draw from J to K.

The length is _____ centimeters.

Complete the table.

	From	Length
4.	A to B	_____ cm
5.	B to C	_____ cm
6.	C to D	_____ cm
7.	D to E	_____ cm
8.	E to A	_____ cm
9.	A to D	_____ cm
10.	C to E	_____ cm

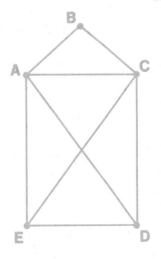

Perfect score: 10   My score: _____

Problem Solving

Solve each problem.

1. Find the length and the width of this rectangle to the nearest centimeter.

It is _____ centimeters long.

It is _____ centimeters wide.

2. The rectangle is how much longer than it is wide?

It is _____ centimeters longer than it is wide.

3. Find the distance around the rectangle.

The distance is _____ centimeters.

4. Draw from A to B, from B to C, and from C to A. Then find the length of each side of the triangle you just drew.

A ·

Side AB is _____ centimeters long.

Side BC is _____ centimeters long.

·B

Side CA is _____ centimeters long.

5. Side CA is how much longer than side BC?

Side CA is _____ centimeters longer.

C ·

6. Find the distance around the triangle.

The distance is _____ centimeters.

7. One side of a square is 8 centimeters long. What is the distance around the square? (All 4 sides of a square are the same length.)

The distance is _____ centimeters.

Perfect score: 10   My score: _____

130

Lesson 3   Liter

is about the same as

1 liter is a little more than 1 quart.

Answer *Yes* or *No*.

1. You can put **1** quart of water in a **1**-liter bottle. _____

2. You can put **3** liters of water in a **3**-quart pail. _____

How many liters would each container hold?
Underline the best answer.

3.

1 liter   8 liters   45 liters

4.

2 liters   9 liters   25 liters

5.

1 liter   10 liters   50 liters

6.

8 liters   28 liters   64 liters

7.

4 liters   16 liters   80 liters

8.

1 liter   4 liters   20 liters

Perfect score: 8   My score: _____

131

Problem Solving

Solve each problem.

1. The tank in Mr. Sumner's car can hold 85 liters. It took 37 liters of gasoline to fill the tank. How many liters were in the tank before it was filled?

_____ liters were in the tank.

2. Mr. Sumner can drive 5 kilometers on each liter of gasoline. How far could he drive on a full tank (85 liters) of gasoline?

He could drive _____ kilometers on a full tank.

3. Miss Gray uses 17 liters of gasoline to drive to and from work each day. How many liters does she use in 6 days?

She uses _____ liters in 6 days.

4. Paul bought 12 liters of paint. The paint was in 3 cans of the same size. How many liters of paint were in each can?

_____ liters of paint were in each can.

5. Connie used 56 liters of water to fill 8 empty fishbowls. The same amount of water was in each bowl. How many liters were in each fishbowl?

_____ liters of water were in each fishbowl.

6. A cafeteria serves 95 liters of milk each day. How much milk is served in 5 days?

_____ liters of milk is served in 5 days.

7. Rosa uses 2 liters of gasoline to mow a lawn. She mowed the lawn 16 times this year. How much gasoline did she use to mow the lawn this year?

Rosa used _____ liters this year.

1.	2.
3.	**4.**
5.	
6.	**7.**

Perfect score: 7   My score: _____

132

CHAPTER 12 TEST

NAME _____

Find each length to the nearest centimeter.

1. _____ cm ════════════════════

2. _____ cm ═══════════════════════

3. _____ cm ══════════

Draw from A to B, from B to C, and from C to A.
Then find each length to the nearest centimeter.

C•

4. From A to B is _____ centimeters.

5. From B to C is _____ centimeters.

6. From C to A is _____ centimeters.

A•   •B

How many liters would each container hold?   Ring the best answer.

7.   8.   9.

1 liter   10 liters   5 liters   500 liters   2 liters   20 liters

Solve each problem.

10. A large carton holds 4 liters of milk. How many liters would 5 of these cartons hold?

Five cartons would hold _____ liters.

11. Karen used an 8-liter sprinkling can to water some plants. She filled the can 4 times. How much water was used?

_____ liters of water was used.

12. A car can go 9 kilometers on 1 liter of gasoline. How far could the car go on 50 liters?

The car could go _____ kilometers.

10.	
11.	12.

Perfect score: 15   My score: _____

133

Find the length of each object to the nearest inch.

1. _____ inches

2. _____ inch

3. _____ inches

Complete the following.

	a		*b*

4. 1 quart = _____ pints   2 quarts = _____ pints

5. 8 pints = _____ quarts   6 pints = _____ quarts

6. 1 gallon = _____ quarts   3 gallons = _____ quarts

7. 8 quarts = _____ gallons   20 quarts = _____ gallons

8. 1 foot = _____ inches   3 feet = _____ inches

9. 1 yard = _____ feet   1 yard = _____ inches

10. 2 weeks = _____ days   1 hour = _____ minutes

11. 4 weeks = _____ days   6 hours = _____ minutes

12. 1 day = _____ hours   2 days = _____ hours

Solve.

13. Annette bought a board that is 6 feet long. What is the length of the board in inches?

It is _____ inches long.

Perfect score: 22   My score: _____

Lesson 1   Inch

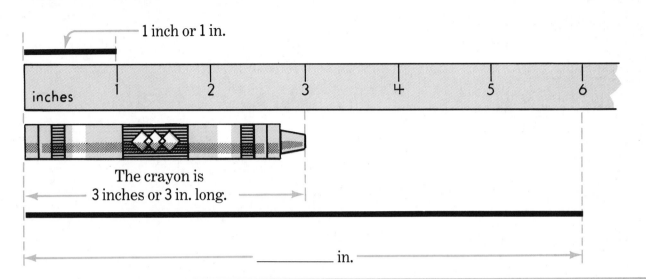

1 inch or 1 in.

inches   1   2   3   4   5   6

The crayon is
3 inches or 3 in. long.

_____ in.

Find the length of each object to the nearest inch.

1. _____ in.

2. _____ in.

3. _____ in.

4. _____ in.

5. _____ in.

Complete the table.

From	Length
6. A to B	_____ in.
7. A to C	_____ in.
8. B to D	_____ in.
9. B to E	_____ in.
10. A to D	_____ in.

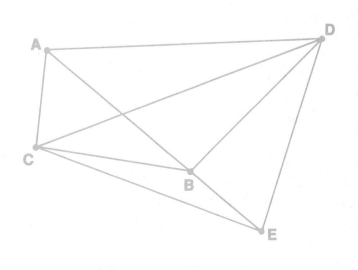

Perfect score: 10   My score: _____

135

Problem Solving

Solve each problem.

1. Find the length and the width of this book to the nearest inch.

It is _____ inches long.

It is _____ inches wide.

2. The book is how much longer than it is wide?

It is _____ inches longer than it is wide.

3. Find the length of this rectangle.

It is _____ inches long.

4. Find the width of this rectangle.

It is _____ inch wide.

5. The rectangle is how much longer than it is wide?

It is _____ inches longer than it is wide.

6. Find the distance around the rectangle.

The distance is _____ inches.

R

7. Draw from R to S, from S to T, and from T to R. Then find the length of each side of the triangle you just drew.

Side RS is _____ inches long.

Side ST is _____ inches long.

Side TR is _____ inches long.

S   T

8. Find the distance around the triangle you drew.

The distance is _____ inches.

Perfect score: 11   My score: _____

136

Lesson 2   Measurement

1 foot (ft) = 12 inches (in.)

3 ft = _____?_____ in.

Since 1 ft = 12 in., then

$$
\begin{array}{cc}
1 & 12 \\
\times 3 & \times 3 \\
\hline
3 & 36
\end{array}
$$

3 ft = _36_ in.

3 feet (ft) = 1 yard (yd)

12 ft = _____?_____ yd

Since 3 ft = 1 yd, then

$$
3\overline{)12} \quad 4
$$

12 ft = _4_ yd

Complete the following.

	a	*b*
1.	6 ft = _____ in.	8 ft = _____ in.
2.	3 yd = _____ ft	8 yd = _____ ft
3.	1 yd = _____ in.	2 yd = _____ in.
4.	21 ft = _____ yd	12 ft = _____ yd
5.	5 yd = _____ ft	14 yd = _____ ft
6.	3 ft = _____ in.	3 yd = _____ in.
7.	7 yd = _____ ft	9 ft = _____ in.
8.	18 ft = _____ yd	11 yd = _____ ft
9.	9 yd = _____ ft	5 ft = _____ in.
10.	7 ft = _____ in.	27 ft = _____ yd
11.	6 yd = _____ ft	15 ft = _____ yd
12.	9 ft = _____ yd	10 yd = _____ ft

Perfect score: 24   My score: _____

Problem Solving

Solve each problem.

1. Teresa bought 2 yards of ribbon for a dress. How many feet of ribbon did she buy?

Teresa bought _____ feet of ribbon.

2. Myron bought a belt that was 2 feet long. How long was the belt in inches?

The belt was _____ inches long.

3. Mark has a rope that is 3 yards long. How long is the rope in feet?

It is _____ feet long.

4. In problem 3, how long is the rope in inches?

It is _____ inches long.

5. Elmer has a piece of wire 5 feet long. How long is the wire in inches?

It is _____ inches long.

6. The distance between 2 walls is 18 feet. What is this distance in yards?

It is _____ yards.

7. Pam's driveway is 15 feet wide. How wide is the driveway in yards?

It is _____ yards wide.

8. A fence post is 4 feet high. How high is the fence post in inches?

It is _____ inches high.

1.	
2.	
3.	
4.	
5.	
6.	
7.	
8.	

Perfect score: 8   My score: _____

138

Lesson 3   Measurement

1 quart (qt) = 2 pints (pt)

5 qt = _?_ pt

Since 1 qt = 2 pt , then

```
    1          2
   ×5         ×5
   ───        ───
    5         10
```

5 qt = _10_ pt

2 pints (pt) = 1 quart (qt)

10 pt = _?_ qt

Since 2 pt = 1 qt , then

10 pt = _5_ qt

1 gallon (gal) = 4 qt or 4 qt = 1 gal

12 qt = _?_ gal

Since 4 qt = 1 gal , then

12 qt = _3_ gal

Complete the following.

	a	b
1.	7 qt = _____ pt	3 qt = _____ pt
2.	8 pt = _____ qt	18 pt = _____ qt
3.	5 gal = _____ qt	2 gal = _____ qt
4.	24 qt = _____ gal	36 qt = _____ gal
5.	4 pt = _____ qt	7 gal = _____ qt
6.	8 qt = _____ pt	20 qt = _____ gal
7.	8 gal = _____ qt	12 pt = _____ qt
8.	28 qt = _____ gal	9 qt = _____ pt
9.	14 pt = _____ qt	9 gal = _____ qt

Perfect score: 18   My score: _____

Problem Solving

Solve each problem.

1. Mrs. Collins bought 12 quarts of milk last week. How many pints of milk was this?

It was _____ pints.

2. In problem **1**, how many gallons of milk did Mrs. Collins buy?

She bought _____ gallons.

3. Mr. Murphy used 24 quarts of paint to paint his house. He bought paint in gallon cans. How many gallons of paint did he use?

He used _____ gallons of paint.

4. Mr. Johnson sold 18 pints of milk yesterday. How many quarts of milk was this?

It was _____ quarts of milk.

5. Warren made 8 quarts of lemonade for a party. How many gallons of lemonade did he make?

He made _____ gallons of lemonade.

6. Maurice drank 10 pints of milk one week. How many quarts of milk did he drink?

He drank _____ quarts of milk.

7. Ms. Carlow used 4 gallons of paint. How many quarts of paint did she use?

She used _____ quarts of paint.

8. How many pint glasses could be filled from 8 quarts of juice?

_____ pint glasses could be filled.

1.	
2.	
3.	
4.	
5.	
6.	
7.	
8.	

Perfect score: 8   My score: _____

140

Lesson 4   Time

3 weeks = _____?_____ days

1 week = 7 days

1
×3
___
3

7
×3
___
21

3 weeks = __21__ days

---

4 hours = _____?_____ min

1 hour = 60 min

4 hours = _____ min

---

2 days = _____?_____ hours

1 day = 24 hours

2 days = _____ hours

Complete the following.

	a	b
1.	2 weeks = _____ days	8 weeks = _____ days
2.	5 hours = _____ min	7 hours = _____ min
3.	6 days = _____ hours	4 days = _____ hours
4.	6 hours = _____ min	9 weeks = _____ days
5.	6 weeks = _____ days	7 days = _____ hours
6.	9 days = _____ hours	3 hours = _____ min
7.	9 hours = _____ min	5 weeks = _____ days
8.	8 days = _____ hours	7 weeks = _____ days

Perfect score: 16   My score: _____

Problem Solving

Solve each problem.

1. Vernon was at camp for 5 weeks. How many days was he at camp?

There are _____ days in 1 week.

He was at camp _____ weeks.

He was at camp _____ days.

2. Esther attends school 6 hours every school day. How many minutes does she attend every school day?

There are _____ minutes in 1 hour.

She attends school _____ hours.

She attends school _____ minutes.

3. Holly was in the hospital for 4 days. How many hours was she in the hospital?

There are _____ hours in 1 day.

Holly was in the hospital _____ days.

She was in the hospital _____ hours.

4. The Cooke family has lived in their new apartment for 6 weeks. How many days have they lived in their new apartment?

They have lived there _____ days.

5. Nancy was away from home for 1 week. How many hours was she away from home?

Nancy was away from home _____ hours.

1.

2.

3.

4.

5.

Perfect score: 11   My score: _____

142

Lesson 5   Problem Solving

Solve each problem.

1. A piece of wire is 2 feet long. How long is the wire in inches?

The wire is _____ inches long.

2. If you use 14 inches of the wire in **1**, how many inches are left?

There will be _____ inches left.

3. On a football field there are 100 yards between goal lines. How many feet is that?

There are _____ feet between goal lines.

4. A container holds 8 quarts of liquid. How many pints does that container hold?

That container holds _____ pints.

5. How many gallons of liquid does the container in **4** hold?

That container holds _____ gallons.

6. A telethon lasted 2 days. How many hours did the telethon last?

The telethon lasted _____ hours.

7. A television mini-series lasted 6 hours. How many minutes did the mini-series last?

The mini-series lasted _____ minutes.

8. The Mohrs spent 3 weeks on their vacation trip. How many days was that?

The vacation trip took _____ days.

1.	2.
3.	4.
5.	6.
7.	8.

Perfect score: 8   My score: _____

143

CHAPTER 13 TEST

Find each length to the nearest inch.

1. _____ in. _____

2. _____ in. _____

3. _____ in. _____

4. _____ in. _____

Complete the following.

a   b

5. 4 ft = _____ in.   4 pt = _____ qt

6. 6 qt = _____ pt   21 ft = _____ yd

7. 8 gal = _____ qt   9 ft = _____ in.

8. 9 yd = _____ ft   36 qt = _____ gal

9. 6 weeks = _____ days   8 hours = _____ min

10. 3 days = _____ hours   8 weeks = _____ days

Solve each problem.

11. Jill has a rope 8 feet long. How long is the rope in inches?

It is _____ inches long.

11.

12. Jim had a gallon of gasoline. He used 1 quart for the lawn mower. How many quarts did he have left?

He had _____ quarts left.

12.

13. Tonya is 4 feet 11 inches tall. What is her height in inches?

Her height is _____ inches.

13.

Perfect score: 19   My score: _____

TEST—Chapters 1–6

Add or subtract.

	a	*b*	*c*	*d*	*e*
1.	6 +5	9 +9	6 1 +5	3 5 +4 3	9 +4 2
2.	8 4 +7	6 4 +1 8	7 0 +7 0	1 8 +9 3	8 5 +8 9
3.	7 0 8 0 +3 0	4 7 8 +5 9 6	2 5 6 1 7 5 +3 1 0	$6.9 8 +7.2 3	$1 1.6 2 3.6 5 +1.9 8
4.	1 6 −7	1 5 −6	3 8 −4	8 7 −1 5	5 6 −8
5.	4 3 −7	8 0 −1 7	1 5 0 −7 0	1 3 6 −6 9	1 8 1 −9 3
6.	8 7 6 −9 7	6 2 5 −2 0 8	8 7 2 4 −8 9 3	$9.8 5 −6.2 7	$1 8.2 0 −6.7 5

For each clockface, write the numerals that name the time.

7.

a	*b*	*c*
_____ : _____	_____ : _____	_____ : _____

Continued on the next page.

Solve each problem.

8. There are 9 bolts in one package. There are 6 bolts in another package. How many bolts are in both packages?

There are _____ bolts in both packages.

9. There are 27 letters to be typed. Only 6 letters have been typed. How many letters still need to be typed?

_____ letters still need to be typed.

8.	9.

10. This morning the temperature was 58°. Now it is 18° warmer. What is the temperature now?

Now the temperature is _____°.

11. Dirk read 84 pages in the morning. He read 69 pages in the afternoon. How many pages did he read that day?

He read _____ pages that day.

10.	11.

12. There were 103 plants in the garden. Only 8 were bean plants. How many were not bean plants?

_____ were not bean plants.

13. You bought items at a store that cost $1.45, $2.98, and $9.98. How much did these items cost altogether?

These items cost $ _____ altogether.

12.	13.

14. Jennifer wants to buy a purse that costs $18.29. She has $9.55. How much more does she need to buy the purse?

She needs $ _____ more.

14.

Perfect score: 40   My score: _____

146

FINAL TEST—Chapters 1–13

Add or subtract.

	a	b	c	d	e

1.

	a	b	c	d	e
	7 +8	6 5 +3	8 2 +1 6	2 6 +9	7 3 +1 9

2.

	2 0 +9 0	6 9 +4 3	1 6 5 +9 2 7	3 6 7 2 +3 5	$2 1.4 3 +6 2.9 7

3.

	1 2 −4	5 6 −5	9 3 −8 3	6 2 −7	8 5 −4 7

4.

	1 8 0 −9 0	1 2 5 −7 6	7 8 0 −5 3 9	3 7 5 1 −8 6 5	$2 5.0 0 −7.2 5

Multiply.

5.

	5 ×3	4 ×4	6 ×5	8 ×3	7 ×2

6.

	3 ×9	8 ×7	6 ×8	9 ×7	6 ×6

Continued on the next page.

Final Test (continued)

Multiply.

	a	*b*	*c*	*d*
7.	7 0 ×5	2 3 ×3	1 8 ×7	4 3 ×7

Divide.

8. 2⟌1 2   4⟌2 0   3⟌2 7   1⟌8

9. 5⟌4 0   4⟌2 4   7⟌0   8⟌7 2

10. 9⟌3 6   7⟌4 9   6⟌4 8   9⟌5 4

Answer each question. Use the calendar to help you.

11.   How many days are in June? _____

12.   On what day is June 17? _____

June

S	M	T	W	T	F	S
				1	2	3
4	5	6	7	8	9	10
11	12	13	14	15	16	17
18	19	20	21	22	23	24
25	26	27	28	29	30	

Continued on the next page.

Final Test (continued)

13. Write the numerals that name the time.

_____ : _____

Find the length to the nearest centimeter.

14. _____ centimeters _____

Find the length to the nearest inch.

15. _____ inches _____

Solve each problem.

16. Juan has 36 inches of wire. How many feet of wire does he have?

    Juan has _____ feet of wire.

16.

17. Caryl used 3 liters of gasoline to mow a lawn. She mowed the lawn 12 times this year. How much gasoline did she use to mow the yard this year?

    She used _____ liters this year.

17.

Continued on the next page.

Final Test (continued)

Solve each problem.

18. Amanda worked in the automobile factory for 45 days. She worked 5 days each week. How many weeks did she work?

Amanda worked _____ weeks.

19. One store sold 421 radios. Another store sold 294 radios. A third store sold 730 radios. How many radios did all three stores sell?

All three stores sold _____ radios.

20. Ms. O'Connor received 1,439 votes. Mr. Ortega received 810 votes. How many more votes did Ms. O'Connor receive than Mr. Ortega?

Ms. O'Connor received _____ more votes.

21. Jack bought 24 liters of paint. The paint was in 6 cans. All the cans were the same size. How many liters of paint were in each can?

There were _____ liters of paint in each can.

22. A farmer has 6 stacks of bales of hay. Each stack has 36 bales. How many bales of hay does the farmer have?

The farmer has _____ bales of hay.

23. Linda bought items that cost $3.80, $2.29, and $1.75. The sales tax was $.47. How much did she pay for those items, including tax?

She paid $ _____.

24. Don had $27.89. He spent $11.92. How much did he have left?

Don had $ _____ left.

18.	19.
20.	21.
22.	23.
24.	

Answers
Math - Grade 3
(Answers for Pre-Tests and Tests are given on pages 157–159.)

Page 3

	a	b	c	d	e	f	g	h
1.	6	4	3	7	4	5	7	6
2.	2	9	8	3	8	7	5	9
3.	8	1	6	4	5	3	9	8
4.	9	6	3	5	9	9	8	7
5.	0	5	8	9	6	2	7	2
6.	9	1	8	6	4	7	6	9

Page 4

	a	b	c	d	e	f	g	h
1.	1	1	0	1	6	2	1	5
2.	5	0	1	1	6	1	3	6
3.	0	6	3	0	2	4	4	2
4.	0	4	8	2	3	1	2	0
5.	2	5	4	3	4	2	0	7
6.	0	1	5	5	9	3	7	2

Page 5

	a	b	c	d	e	f
1.	11	10	9	12	11	9
2.	10	12	8	7	10	10
3.	8	12	12	10	11	10
4.	12	9	11	10	7	12
5.	7	9	10	11	11	12
6.	8	10	11	8	11	8

Page 6

1. 2 ; 9 ; 11   3. 7 ; 4 ; 11   5. 12
2. 8 ; 4 ; 12   4. 4 ; 6 ; 10

Page 7

	a	b	c	d	e	f
1.	4	6	2	3	3	9
2.	9	3	3	5	9	3
3.	5	3	6	2	8	5
4.	2	4	4	4	6	0
5.	6	1	1	1	7	2
6.	8	4	7	7	5	8

Page 8

1. 12 ; 3 ; 9   3. 10 ; 7 ; 3   5. 7
2. 11 ; 8 ; 3   4. 11 ; 2 ; 9

Page 9

	a	b	c	d	e	f
1.	11	12	10	11	10	12
2.	12	11	12	10	11	10
3.	2	5	8	6	4	3
4.	2	4	3	7	4	7

Page 10

1. add ; 11   3. subtract ; 7   5. add ; 10
2. subtract ; 2   4. add ; 12   6. subtract ; 5

Page 11

	a	b	c	d	e	f
1.	13	15	11	16	13	16
2.	14	10	14	13	12	15
3.	15	10	13	11	14	10
4.	12	17	15	11	13	18
5.	16	10	17	13	10	11
6.	14	12	11	12	14	12

Page 12

1. 9 ; 7 ; 16   3. 13   5. 16
2. 6 ; 9 ; 15   4. 17   6. 13

Page 13

	a	b	c	d	e	f
1.	8	6	9	1	7	8
2.	9	6	8	9	7	7
3.	4	9	9	3	7	4
4.	8	5	5	9	6	5
5.	5	3	9	6	8	3
6.	8	7	8	5	7	7

Page 14

1. 13 ; 5 ; 8   3. 9   5. 8
2. 18 ; 9 ; 9   4. 7   6. 8

Page 15

	a	b	c	d	e	f
1.	14	16	12	11	17	10
2.	13	12	15	13	10	14
3.	6	9	8	9	8	5
4.	7	8	9	7	8	5

Page 16

1. add ; 16   3. subtract ; 9   5. subtract ; 9
2. add ; 14   4. subtract ; 8

Page 19

	a	b	c	d	e	f
1.	8	28	5	45	6	26
2.	7	67	9	59	7	87
3.	6	16	26	36	46	56
4.	68	37	27	94	58	43
5.	44	23	66	86	27	18
6.	59	66	28	39	53	48
7.	38	47	53	68	26	36

Page 20

1. 37   3. 48   5. 18   7. 24
2. 29   4. 28   6. 15

Page 21

	a	b	c	d	e	f
1.	68	84	67	91	77	85
2.	89	66	86	83	59	97
3.	56	66	58	91	95	72
4.	87	88	39	67	76	88
5.	55	84	69	84	36	66
6.	59	87	59	78	68	46

Page 22

1. 25   3. 97   5. 67   7. 89
2. 55   4. 86   6. 78

Page 23

	a	b	c	d	e	f
1.	6	46	3	33	6	86
2.	6	76	1	61	0	80
3.	42	32	73	40	30	61
4.	23	21	35	18	33	53
5.	31	38	21	30	61	14
6.	57	36	20	20	22	71
7.	15	22	62	31	67	63

Page 24

1. 21   3. 14   5. 51   7. 30
2. 92   4. 50   6. 61

151

Page 25

	a	b	c	d	e	f
1.	25	13	62	55	23	33
2.	60	16	32	61	10	11
3.	51	32	51	15	10	53
4.	43	63	23	34	25	61

Page 26

1. 31 3. 50 5. 13 7. 75
2. 25 4. 16 6. 34

Page 27

	a	b	c	d	e	f
1.	58	93	56	66	95	87
2.	68	58	78	52	78	69
3.	55	35	11	32	43	22
4.	14	20	29	22	26	23

Page 28

1. 23 3. 36 5. 12 7. 49
2. 32 4. 23 6. 64

Page 31

	a	b	c	d	e	f
1.	32	43	91	47	50	51
2.	54	34	45	85	33	46
3.	30	51	44	38	64	51
4.	83	50	30	31	23	28
5.	21	50	60	74	45	22
6.	37	43	61	43	51	47
7.	54	34	76	63	90	85

Page 32

1. 44 ; 8 ; 52 3. 25 5. 91
2. 72 ; 9 ; 81 4. 76

Page 33

	a	b	c	d	e	f
1.	62	85	80	64	72	91
2.	57	75	72	90	98	81
3.	84	63	84	73	72	94
4.	97	63	92	46	62	56
5.	73	52	75	91	74	96
6.	92	73	86	81	70	62
7.	91	75	70	88	83	83

Page 34

1. 31 ; 29 ; 60 3. 29 ; 13 ; 42 5. 61
2. 46 ; 36 ; 82 4. 77

Page 35

	a	b	c	d	e	f
1.	45	18	37	49	26	58
2.	19	39	29	37	59	83
3.	46	58	55	68	41	37
4.	88	67	73	39	59	42
5.	86	79	29	18	38	57
6.	14	68	36	35	46	18
7.	39	24	74	68	84	55

Page 36

1. 48 ; 9 ; 39 3. 38 5. 66
2. 91 ; 5 ; 86 4. 44 6. 78

Page 37

	a	b	c	d	e	f
1.	18	8	17	37	25	9
2.	18	17	14	38	8	66
3.	28	8	7	19	16	9
4.	28	17	7	27	19	13
5.	58	78	26	56	52	57
6.	9	35	29	25	12	46
7.	34	37	8	49	27	46

Page 38

1. 95 ; 26 ; 69 3. 39 5. 27
2. 73 ; 45 ; 28 4. 12 6. 15

Page 39

	a	b	c	d	e	f
1.	61	55	81	85	70	91
2.	64	56	50	76	94	73
3.	54	39	19	67	38	38
4.	18	49	48	35	28	14

Page 40

1. subtract ; 8 3. add ; 91 5. add ; 54
2. subtract ; 17 4. subtract ; 18

Page 43

	a	b	c	d	e	f
1.	15	150	15	150	11	110
2.	12	120	17	170	10	100
3.	110	140	120	140	130	120
4.	110	120	130	100	160	160
5.	8	80	9	90	6	60
6.	9	90	9	90	9	90
7.	60	40	80	70	80	70
8.	40	90	70	40	50	70

Page 44

1. subtract ; 80 3. subtract ; 60 5. 120
2. add ; 120 4. 20 6. 60

Page 45

	a	b	c	d	e	f
1.	136	149	109	129	118	118
2.	115	148	129	126	157	113
3.	122	156	185	107	115	116
4.	107	136	176	136	186	126
5.	139	156	126	107	160	165
6.	177	119	117	108	125	142
7.	138	105	146	127	188	177

Page 46

1. 96 ; 81 ; 177 3. 83 ; 84 ; 167 5. 148
2. 53 ; 85 ; 138 4. 139

Page 47

	a	b	c	d	e	f
1.	83	36	73	85	94	72
2.	50	91	27	42	93	62
3.	66	81	93	43	13	94
4.	84	67	94	60	94	63
5.	91	71	81	77	47	42
6.	53	56	80	74	73	52
7.	35	91	72	72	50	93

Page 48

1. 128 ; 73 ; 55 3. 167 ; 71 ; 96 5. 91
2. 145 ; 75 ; 70 4. 65

Page 49

	a	b	c	d	e	f
1.	127	127	156	114	106	114
2.	173	116	147	127	128	104
3.	92	92	71	94	84	57
4.	74	82	81	67	95	83

Page 50

1. add ; 120 3. add ; 153
2. subtract ; 38

152

Page 51

	a	b	c	d	e	f
1.	162	123	134	110	142	151
2.	172	131	112	125	130	185
3.	156	148	111	122	161	147
4.	110	122	131	153	142	114
5.	134	126	191	160	153	113
6.	142	152	187	111	125	146

Page 52

1. 74 ; 87 ; 161   3. 84 ; 48 ; 132   5. 134
2. 49 ; 57 ; 106   4. 180

Page 53

	a	b	c	d	e	f
1.	49	89	86	77	83	68
2.	37	44	72	85	89	67
3.	87	88	39	69	58	78
4.	58	67	88	73	67	88
5.	58	58	76	57	59	69
6.	64	87	68	47	75	86
7.	79	78	69	89	59	23

Page 54

1. 180 ; 95 ; 85   3. 162 ; 84 ; 78   5. 47
2. 128 ; 79 ; 49   4. 97

Page 55

	a	b	c	d	e	f
1.	92	127	143	119	79	84
2.	168	132	129	70	78	110
3.	33	141	78	60	70	48
4.	65	85	131	115	99	70
5.	159	58	79	60	87	69

Page 56

1. 166 ; 98 ; 68   3. 84 ; 39 ; 123   5. 77
2. 115 ; 27 ; 88   4. 152

Page 59

	a	b	c	d	e	f
1.	16	23	15	20	15	20
2.	130	190	160	160	160	220
3.	136	183	165	160	165	220
4.	98	104	165	104	149	127
5.	121	174	142	234	103	92
6.	115	148	178	134	130	149

Page 60

1. 72 ; 69 ; 64 ; 205   3. 217
2. 55 ; 68 ; 79 ; 202   4. 146

Page 61

	a	b	c	d	e	f
1.	1002	819	703	773	864	471
2.	1769	1262	998	997	1485	1579
3.	1521	1808	1042	1402	1563	935
4.	959	902	1789	994	1995	1961
5.	1395	1466	1495	1820	1243	1803

Page 62

1. 175 ; 142 ; 327 ; 644   3. 991
2. 768 ; 829 ; 107 ; 1704   4. 507

Page 63

	a	b	c	d	e	f
1.	261	109	319	189	189	120
2.	91	548	307	299	209	42
3.	627	188	379	628	209	205
4.	579	688	591	269	387	608
5.	482	252	321	582	99	394
6.	497	150	419	414	190	109

Page 64

1. 714 ; 521 ; 193   3. 726 ; 340 ; 386   5. 175
2. 850 ; 317 ; 533   4. 109

Page 65

	a	b	c	d	e
1.	7332	6411	7122	4210	2002
2.	3327	4106	6003	3218	5157
3.	3370	9371	3363	5034	3470
4.	3571	3202	7811	4910	5500
5.	5449	1584	3749	2949	1806
6.	7854	6775	2999	3469	854

Page 66

1. 3165 ; 875 ; 2290   3. 937   5. 1355
2. 4418 ; 979 ; 3439   4. 4385   6. 659

Page 69

	a	b	a	b
1.	31	Friday	4. 18th	11th
2.	5	5	5. 120	November 10
3.	4	7		

Page 70

	a		b	
1.	5	3	10	7
2.	20	10	25	12
3.	45	8	15	9
4.	30	5	30	6
5.	10	1	5	1

	a	b	c	d
6.	6:05	2:45	7:20	8:35
7.	3:30	1:25	9:40	10:15

Page 71

	a	b	c	d
1.		20	12	8
2.	4	26	17	31
3.	36	29	11	33
4.	18	9	34	13
5.	5	25	6	21
6.	38	35	27	16
7.	23	37	14	32

	a	b	c
8.	III	VII	XV
9.	XIX	XXII	XXVIII
10.	XXX	XX	XXXIX

Page 72

1. 10 ; 2   6. 14 ; 5
2. 10 ; 1   7. 12 ; 70
3. 20 ; 2   8. 8 ; 14
4. 15 ; 3   9. 0 ; 65
5. 20 ; 4   10. 10 ; 1

Page 73

	a	b	c	d	e
1.	$12.76	$ 5.21	$41.36	95¢	$ 4.62
2.	$ 2.02	$ 7.56	$ 2.46	12¢	$22.74
3.	$22.02	$12.07	$20.79	90¢	$18.05
4.	$11.78	$ 3.62	$10.44	16¢	$13.14
5.	$13.55	$69.01	$ 2.00	28¢	$ 1.22
6.	$45.47	$33.04	$ 2.28	73¢	$ 9.39

Page 74

1. $40.62   3. $.75   5. $7.15   7. 27¢
2. $51.72   4. $10.64 ; $6.29   6. $5.77

153

Page 77

1.	two times five	4. four times eight
2.	three times four	5. four times seven
3.	five times two	

	a	b
6.	4 + 4	2 + 2 + 2 + 2
7.	5 + 5 + 5	3 + 3 + 3 + 3 + 3
8.	7 + 7 + 7	3 + 3 + 3 + 3 + 3 + 3 + 3
9.	6 + 6 + 6 + 6	4 + 4 + 4 + 4 + 4 + 4
10.	8 + 8	2 + 2 + 2 + 2 + 2 + 2 + 2 + 2
11.	9 + 9 + 9	3 + 3 + 3 + 3 + 3 + 3 + 3 + 3 + 3

Page 78

	a	b	c	d	e	f
1.	16	16	8	8	10	10
2.	12	12	14	14	4	4
3.	18	18	6	6	2	2
4.	6	6	9	9	12	12
5.	15	15	18	18	21	21
6.	24	24	27	27	3	3

Page 79

	a	b	c	d	e	f
1.	0	9	7	0	5	0
2.	0	8	4	0	0	6
3.	0	0	5	6	1	0
4.	7	0	0	0	7	5
5.	0	9	6	0	0	2
6.	4	8	0	8	0	0
7.	0	6	0	9	0	3
8.	2	0	0	3	4	0

Page 80

1. 2 ; 9 ; 18   3. 24
2. 2 ; 6 ; 12   4. 40

Page 81

	a	b	c	d	e	f
1.	20	32	35	30	8	12
2.	25	18	36	4	0	16
3.	15	28	10	8	40	18
4.	15	9	16	0	6	10
5.	24	24	4	0	5	12
6.	45	0	12	14	21	5

Page 82

1. 5 ; 9 ; 45   3. 7 ; 4 ; 28   5. 20
2. 7 ; 5 ; 35   4. 5 ; 3 ; 15

Page 83

	a	b	c	d	e	f
1.	0	8	40	21	6	0
2.	1	18	16	15	30	4
3.	0	2	0	16	45	25
4.	32	18	5	0	2	14
5.	15	28	20	6	27	8
6.	0	3	12	0	6	36
7.	35	24	0	0	4	24
8.	20	4	9	7	8	9
9.	9	0	10	12	10	12

Page 84

1. 6 ; 1 ; 6   3. 40   5. 30
2. 8 ; 4 ; 32   4. 10   6. 12

Page 87

	a	b	c	d	e	f
1.	30	9	54	32	0	15
2.	40	12	24	25	12	6
3.	12	28	30	48	36	24
4.	0	18	5	16	6	20
5.	42	45	35	0	10	8
6.	36	12	20	3	15	0
7.	4	10	6	27	21	24

Page 88

1. 6 ; 4 ; 24   3. 6 ; 9 ; 54
2. 8 ; 6 ; 48

Page 89

	a	b	c	d	e	f
1.	49	42	48	21	72	0
2.	64	40	8	21	24	7
3.	0	48	40	63	7	42
4.	56	35	0	14	35	0
5.	56	16	32	28	24	32
6.	36	8	28	16	14	54

Page 90

1. 7 ; 9 ; 63   3. 8 ; 7 ; 56   5. 42
2. 4 ; 7 ; 28   4. 35

Page 91

	a	b	c	d	e	f
1.	63	54	64	21	18	21
2.	40	56	36	48	0	49
3.	81	8	0	54	56	16
4.	32	0	28	18	32	42
5.	40	63	24	9	7	0
6.	45	0	27	35	72	14

Page 92

1. 8 ; 9 ; 72   3. 45   5. 54
2. 9 ; 9 ; 81   4. 36   6. 63

Page 93

	a	b	c	d	e	f
1.	63	42	5	18	18	64
2.	21	36	0	35	56	36
3.	45	24	45	16	56	0
4.	42	6	72	0	25	63
5.	40	32	28	0	9	20
6.	48	54	30	24	49	27
7.	48	40	28	15	81	7
8.	36	35	8	72	30	10
9.	12	0	54	24	32	14

Page 94

1. 5 ; 8 ; 40   3. 6 ; 9 ; 54   5. 72
2. 9 ; 9 ; 81   4. 42   6. 56

Page 97

	a	b	c	d	e	f
1.	6	60	8	80	6	60
2.	80	80	90	30	90	70
3.	36	360	18	180	25	250
4.	210	300	160	100	240	540
5.	80	150	120	40	180	280
6.	490	240	70	640	90	240
7.	200	160	120	150	50	40
8.	420	250	240	180	560	270

Page 98

1. 30 ; 4 ; 120   3. 30 ; 3 ; 90   5. 80
2. 20 ; 2 ; 40   4. 180   6. 280

Page 99

	a	b	c	d	e	f
1.	124	219	368	168	106	126
2.	46	93	84	48	99	84
3.	84	183	102	86	328	39
4.	216	96	129	69	68	186

Answers Grade 3

Page 100

	a	b	c	d	e	f
1.	248	168	219	164	182	156
2.	86	164	96	183	168	88
3.	216	213	162	129	208	166
4.	124	279	52	148	106	186
5.	288	405	276	189	108	146
6.	427	128	246	729	126	455
7.	159	426	328	819	368	648

Page 101

	a	b	c	d	e	f
1.	92	87	80	98	78	96
2.	74	52	94	84	75	96
3.	90	70	84	70	92	76
4.	90	81	90	84	60	96
5.	56	72	85	78	57	76
6.	72	72	75	64	58	54

Page 102

1. 12 ; 7 ; 84   3. 98
2. 14 ; 5 ; 70   4. 72

Page 103

	a	b	c	d	e	f
1.	140	252	168	235	228	125
2.	216	162	190	384	581	444
3.	300	174	184	222	145	138
4.	336	558	496	285	156	154
5.	270	476	657	696	564	332
6.	480	255	188	207	273	390

Page 104

1. 25 ; 9 ; 225   3. 36 ; 7 ; 252   5. 108
2. 26 ; 6 ; 156   4. 200

Page 107

1.	10	5		6.	24	8	
2.	21	7		7.	3	21	7
3.	4	2		8.	2	4	2
4.	18	6		9.	2	10	5
5.	18	9		10.	3	18	6

Page 108

	a				b			
1.			5	5			2	2
2.		2	4	4		8	2	2
3.	4	2	2	2	4	2	2	2

Page 109

	a	b
1.	5	6
2.	7	8
3.	1	3
4.	8	9

	a	b	c	d
5.	5	3	1	2
6.	7	9	4	6

Page 110

1. 24 ; 3 ; 8   3. 16 ; 2 ; 8   5. 9
2. 8 ; 2 ; 4   4. 9

Page 111

	a	b
1.	7	6
2.	4	3
3.	6	4
4.	9	8

	a	b	c	d
5.	2	2	1	3
6.	5	1	8	7

Page 112

1. 24 ; 4 ; 6   3. 32 ; 4 ; 8   5. 9
2. 28 ; 4 ; 7   4. 5

Page 113

	a	b
1.	5	14
2.	4	9

	a	b	c	d	e
3.	4	3	12	2	16
4.	4	6	9	3	2
5.	4	7	9	1	9
6.	8	3	5	7	18
7.	1	5	2	6	8

Page 114

1. 16 ; 2 ; 8   3. 36 ; 4 ; 9   5. 5
2. 9 ; 3 ; 3   4. 7

Page 117

	a	b
1.	2	1
2.	5	7
3.	8	9

	a	b	c	d
4.	1	2	6	3
5.	6	0	4	7
6.	5	9	8	9
7.	8	4	5	6

Page 118

1. 30 ; 6 ; 5   3. 18 ; 6 ; 3   5. 4
2. 12 ; 6 ; 2   4. 1

Page 119

	a	b
1.	2	3
2.	5	4
3.	7	8

	a	b	c	d
4.	1	0	2	4
5.	6	6	1	8
6.	0	7	7	9
7.	8	5	9	3

Page 120

1. 28 ; 7 ; 4   3. 3   5. 1
2. 48 ; 8 ; 6   4. 2

Page 121

	a	b
1.	5	3
2.	8	4
3.	6	9

	a	b	c	d
4.	1	9	2	4
5.	0	8	6	9
6.	9	7	6	5
7.	3	7	9	7

Page 122

1. 54 ; 9 ; 6   3. 4   5. 5
2. 27 ; 9 ; 3   4. 2

Page 123

	a	b	c	d
1.	5	6	1	8
2.	3	2	4	6
3.	9	8	5	0
4.	5	8	3	6
5.	2	5	1	8
6.	2	2	4	3
7.	4	3	3	2
8.	8	7	5	5
9.	7	5	7	8
10.	8	6	6	9

Page 124

1. 42 ; 6 ; 7   2. 63 ; 7 ; 9   3. 64 ; 8 ; 8

Page 127

1. 1   3. 5   5. 8
2. 3   4. 11   6. 4

Answers Grade 3

Page 128
1. 28
2. 21
3. 7
4. 2
5. 16
6.–10. Answers vary.

Page 129
1. 8
2. 6
3. 5
4. 2
5. 2
6. 4
7. 3
8. 4
9. 5
10. 5

Page 130
1. 7 ; 3
2. 4
3. 20
4. 4 ; 5 ; 7
5. 2
6. 16
7. 32

Page 131
1. Yes
2. No
3. 1 liter
4. 2 liters
5. 10 liters
6. 8 liters
7. 4 liters
8. 20 liters

Page 132
1. 48
2. 425
3. 102
4. 4
5. 7
6. 475
7. 32

Page 135
1. 3
2. 2
3. 4
4. 5
5. 1
6. 2
7. 1
8. 2
9. 1
10. 3

Page 136
1. 11 ; 8
2. 3
3. 4
4. 1
5. 3
6. 10
7. 2 ; 1 ; 2
8. 5

Page 137

	a	b			a	b
1.	72	96		7.	21	108
2.	9	24		8.	6	33
3.	36	72		9.	27	60
4.	7	4		10.	84	9
5.	15	42		11.	18	5
6.	36	108		12.	3	30

Page 138
1. 6
2. 24
3. 9
4. 108
5. 60
6. 6
7. 5
8. 48

Page 139

	a	b		a	b		a	b
1.	14	6	4.	6	9	7.	32	6
2.	4	9	5.	2	28	8.	7	18
3.	20	8	6.	16	5	9.	7	36

Page 140
1. 24
2. 3
3. 6
4. 9
5. 2
6. 5
7. 16
8. 16

Page 141

	a	b		a	b		a	b
1.	14	56	4.	360	63	7.	540	35
2.	300	420	5.	42	168	8.	192	49
3.	144	96	6.	216	180			

Page 142
1. 7 ; 5 ; 35
2. 60 ; 6 ; 360
3. 24 ; 4 ; 96
4. 42
5. 168

Page 143
1. 24
2. 10
3. 300
4. 16
5. 2
6. 48
7. 360
8. 21

156

Page vii

	a	b	c	d	e	f	g	h
1.	4	10	7	11	9	10	9	16
2.	10	9	12	3	5	2	10	5
3.	9	15	12	12	4	8	4	8
4.	7	11	6	15	8	10	9	13
5.	5	9	7	11	2	16	8	12
6.	17	6	14	12	11	6	10	8
7.	14	5	9	15	0	17	11	12
8.	6	3	13	7	10	1	14	12
9.	13	7	18	7	13	11	11	10
10.	16	14	10	13	14	11	13	15

Page viii

	a	b	c	d	e	f	g	h
1.	10	7	1	2	10	7	13	9
2.	1	9	3	5	8	9	11	10
3.	5	3	12	8	14	12	13	11
4.	6	14	13	8	13	17	0	8
5.	9	16	8	11	16	14	6	9
6.	4	9	4	6	14	6	14	13
7.	12	12	5	11	11	11	10	9
8.	2	10	12	4	15	10	7	10
9.	17	11	7	8	10	12	18	13
10.	12	15	15	8	15	16	11	10

Page ix

	a	b	c	d	e	f	g	h
1.	8	4	0	9	1	1	1	2
2.	5	0	3	7	1	4	7	8
3.	9	9	1	6	8	6	0	9
4.	5	2	0	3	2	8	5	4
5.	9	1	2	6	2	8	0	2
6.	6	1	1	4	6	8	2	7
7.	7	5	4	4	2	7	2	5
8.	7	6	1	5	3	3	0	7
9.	9	0	8	8	2	5	0	7
10.	9	3	3	9	9	8	6	6

Page x

	a	b	c	d	e	f	g	h
1.	2	6	1	9	1	7	9	3
2.	6	7	3	2	1	2	6	9
3.	4	8	8	9	5	6	5	1
4.	2	4	1	7	4	8	8	1
5.	0	9	4	8	3	6	7	5
6.	0	8	1	6	4	3	5	7
7.	2	5	7	7	5	7	9	6
8.	0	7	3	8	5	5	9	6
9.	5	6	0	9	1	4	8	8
10.	3	4	0	9	4	4	8	7

Page xi

	a	b	c	d	e	f	g	h
1.	4	18	0	6	0	1	7	32
2.	28	0	24	2	5	18	10	12
3.	21	25	48	0	36	9	14	12
4.	40	8	35	4	16	30	56	9
5.	0	8	27	30	24	18	35	18
6.	63	24	32	21	54	36	12	56
7.	3	45	15	64	20	0	12	42
8.	15	0	14	49	40	54	0	36
9.	81	8	48	0	63	0	27	72
10.	24	72	16	28	6	42	9	45

Page xii

	a	b	c	d	e	f	g	h
1.	4	24	4	49	0	18	0	4
2.	0	3	24	27	0	54	21	32
3.	2	36	18	14	35	5	16	16
4.	32	45	8	6	54	28	12	30
5.	8	7	9	12	36	5	48	42
6.	28	1	40	40	0	0	6	27
7.	24	63	10	12	12	72	35	42
8.	48	20	24	18	7	8	16	15
9.	30	56	81	0	21	25	10	64
10.	9	20	56	36	72	63	14	45

Page xiii

	a	b	c	d	e	f	g
1.	1	6	2	6	4	2	4
2.	0	9	3	8	3	0	1
3.	5	5	4	5	9	7	4
4.	2	4	1	9	4	2	5
5.	3	2	7	5	8	9	6
6.	8	5	6	1	0	2	1
7.	6	5	8	3	4	9	2
8.	5	4	0	7	6	0	7
9.	0	8	7	8	8	3	6
10.	7	1	2	0	7	3	5
11.	3	7	8	6	2	9	1
12.	9	8	9	3	6	4	9

Page xiv

	a	b	c	d	e	f	g
1.	1	3	3	4	6	2	0
2.	5	4	2	2	1	8	9
3.	7	0	9	5	2	9	7
4.	1	4	8	7	1	1	6
5.	0	4	8	6	3	3	9
6.	3	4	3	0	9	0	2
7.	0	5	5	1	9	5	6
8.	2	5	7	6	8	7	5
9.	0	1	8	7	1	6	2
10.	6	5	4	8	7	6	6
11.	8	4	4	2	9	7	3
12.	3	7	9	8	4	9	8

Page 1

	a	b	c	d	e	f
1.	10	12	13	10	14	17
2.	11	13	10	18	10	15
3.	16	14	13	10	12	12
4.	11	12	11	14	16	15
5.	7	4	9	9	9	8
6.	8	8	9	8	4	8
7.	5	6	9	8	8	2
8.	7	9	9	9	8	4
9.	3	7	7	6	7	7

Page 2

1. 2 ; 2 ; 4   2. 1 ; 2 ; 3   3. 5 ; 2 ; 3

Page 17

	a	b	c	d	e	f
1.	15	13	11	10	14	12
2.	10	13	12	11	16	14
3.	12	15	11	17	11	13
4.	15	13	18	12	16	10
5.	13	12	10	11	10	14

	a	b	c	d	e
6.	4	7	9	8	4
7.	9	9	2	5	7
8.	8	8	5	5	8
9.	8	4	7	6	7

157

Answers

Page 18

	a	b	c	d	e	f
1.	9	49	5	55	7	87
2.	59	27	47	27	45	26
3.	35	48	66	46	17	27
4.	85	38	78	88	75	35
5.	63	48	97	39	68	53
6.	3	33	3	43	2	32
7.	34	21	51	22	66	23
8.	31	45	16	64	72	50
9.	15	20	61	33	10	27

Page 29

	a	b	c	d	e	f
1.	6	26	39	25	76	39
2.	57	79	87	67	85	87
3.	5	35	41	23	41	22
4.	25	41	23	40	32	37
5.	58					

Page 30

	a	b	c	d	e	f
1.	59	26	37	89	67	27
2.	41	62	47	61	56	33
3.	75	86	77	89	59	78
4.	81	71	97	73	75	78
5.	72	79	64	96	66	93
6.	34	25	50	85	51	83
7.	38	67	38	46	35	27
8.	42	12	11	23	12	48
9.	48	36	68	8	29	50

Page 41

	a	b	c	d	e	f
1.	43	54	31	24	52	64
2.	42	74	81	93	96	81
3.	18	45	58	18	48	57
4.	19	28	19	48	4	25
5.	81					

Page 42

	a	b	c	d	e	f
1.	11	110	15	150	170	140
2.	148	118	178	137	107	159
3.	141	171	124	131	176	141
4.	79	91	139	126	99	148
5.	118	88	150	126	133	80
6.	9	90	6	60	80	90
7.	83	91	64	93	97	80
8.	49	89	87	86	67	77
9.	123	149	82	79	114	67

Page 57

	a	b	c	d	e
1.	140	160	148	126	125
2.	141	140	181	156	123
3.	90	80	82	45	84
4.	68	78	77	88	65
5.	111	93	90	146	124

Page 58

	a	b	c	d	e	f
1.	14	23	21	22	21	24
2.	130	150	190	190	180	140
3.	123	148	134	153	191	107
4.	99	112	198	183	218	115
5.	848	987	826	1250	1588	1016

	a	b	c	d	e
6.	411	249	390	276	276
7.	4502	5359	3761	6899	5838

Page 67

	a	b	c	d	e
1.	10	17	21	190	230
2.	79	98	192	155	229
3.	881	959	847	1269	1876
4.	522	107	492	549	
5.	5522	7267	5771	1796	
6.	974				
7.	2438				

Page 68

	a	b	c
1.	365	4	
2.	366	4	
3.	30	45	
4.	31	15	
5.		5	4
6.	17	26	19
7.		X	IX
8.	XXIV	XXXI	XXV

	a	b	c	d	e
9.	$12.09	$13.90	83¢	94¢	$18.51
10.	$13.25	$11.85	$6.56	18¢	47¢
11.	$33.32				

Page 75

1.	31	2. Friday	

	a	b	c
3.	7:05	10:45	12:30
4.		9	32
5.		VIII	XXIX

	a	b	c	d	e
6.	$31.77	$3.97	96¢	73¢	$15.70
7.	$ 1.35	$7.81	54¢	$16.41	$ 4.06
8.	$ 3.93				

Page 76

	a	b	c	d	e	f
1.	10	14	4	12	8	18
2.	9	15	12	21	27	6
3.	0	0	0	0	0	0
4.	3	7	4	1	5	8
5.	28	12	36	24	20	16
6.	40	30	45	20	15	10
7.	0	32	18	0	25	0
8.	9	8	2	35	24	2
9.	6	3	0	16	6	5

Page 85

	a	b	c	d	e
1.	6	28	0	12	45
2.	12	21	0	4	12
3.	18	40	27	6	16
4.	0	25	36	0	20
5.	5 ; 6 ; 30				
6.	32				
7.	24				

Page 86

	a	b	c	d	e	f
1.	42	36	24	48	30	54
2.	56	28	63	49	42	35
3.	72	40	56	64	48	32
4.	54	81	45	72	36	63
5.	81					
6.	56					
7.	63					
8.	42					

Page 95

	a	b	c	d	e
1.	42	45	48	28	49
2.	63	81	7	24	63
3.	0	56	40	72	42
4.	72	32	54	14	27
5.	6 ; 9 ; 54				
6.	64				
7.	24				

Page 96

	a	b	c	d	e	f
1.	6	60	8	80	7	70
2.	96	48	39	84	55	69
3.	28	280	18	180	36	360
4.	186	148	248	248	166	205
5.	72	78	70	72	76	80
6.	172	135	105	276	168	270
7.	392	126	400	46	74	225
8.	68	320	219	66	162	162
9.	270	232	112	75	320	132

Page 105

	a	b	c	d	e
1.	60	84	69	240	240
2.	168	219	147	84	81
3.	285	228	210	116	180
4.	60	146	174	360	84
5.	4 ; 52 ; 208				
6.	148				
7.	84				

Page 106

	a	b	c	d	e
1.	3	6	9	2	5
2.	4	8	3	5	1
3.	4	8	16	9	27
4.	8	1	9	6	21
5.	12	4	7	2	14
6.	5	7	1	2	6
7.	6				
8.	4				
9.	6				

Page 115

	a	b	c	d	e	
1.	5	4	1	3	8	5. 45 ; 5 ; 9
2.	12	6	4	7	5	6. 7
3.	2	8	4	9	8	7. 3
4.	8	1	10	9	6	

Page 116

	a	b	c	d	e
1.	4	2	3	0	1
2.	7	9	5	6	8
3.	0	4	2	3	1
4.	8	6	9	5	7
5.	1	5	0	4	2
6.	3	6	8	9	7
7.	4	3	5	2	0
8.	8	7	6	1	9
9.	1	7	1	6	3

Page 125

	a	b	c	d	e
1.	2	1	3	6	0
2.	2	5	7	4	9
3.	8	3	5	2	9
4.	8	9	8	9	3
5.	5	4	8	9	6

6. 24 ; 6 ; 4   7. 3

Page 126

1. 4	4. 3	7. False
2. 10	5. 6	8. True
3. 8	6. False	9. 330

Page 133

1. 5	3. 3	5. 5
2. 9	4. 4	6. 3

7. 1 liter	10. 20
8. 500 liters	11. 32
9. 2 liters	12. 450

Page 134

1. 3   2. 1   3. 4

	a	b		a	b
4.	2	4	9.	3	36
5.	4	3	10.	14	60
6.	4	12	11.	28	360
7.	2	5	12.	24	48
8.	12	36	13.	72	

Page 144

1. 4   2. 1   3. 3   4. 2

	a	b		a	b
5.	48	2	8.	27	9
6.	12	7	9.	42	480
7.	32	108	10.	72	56

11. 96   12. 3   13. 59

Page 145

	a	b	c	d	e
1.	11	18	66	78	51
2.	91	82	140	111	174
3.	180	1074	741	$14.21	$17.25
4.	9	9	34	72	48
5.	36	63	80	67	88
6.	779	417	7831	$ 3.58	$11.45

	a	b	c
7.	8:00	3:30	6:10

Page 146

8. 15	11. 153	13. 14.41
9. 21	12. 95	14. 8.74
10. 76		

Page 147

	a	b	c	d	e
1.	15	68	98	35	92
2.	110	112	1092	143	$84.40
3.	8	51	10	55	38
4.	90	49	241	2886	$17.75
5.	15	16	30	24	14
6.	27	56	48	63	36

Page 148

	a	b	c	d
7.	350	69	126	301
8.	6	5	9	8
9.	8	6	0	9
10.	4	7	8	6
11.	30			
12.	Saturday			

Page 149

13. 11:20	14. 9	16. 3
	15. 2	17. 36

Page 150

18. 9	21. 4	23. 8.31
19. 1445	22. 216	24. 15.97
20. 629		